Lucille K. Lovestedt

Doing Eighty

Other Books by Lucille Lovestedt:

Reclaiming Functional Communication
Commission of Child and Animal Protection

11525 Betty Way
Grass Valley, CA 95949
lucillelovestedt@gmail.com
http://lucillelovestedt.wordpress.com/

TABLE OF CONTENTS

In Loving Memory of
Ward Lovestedt
and
David Lovestedt

Dedicated To:
Barbara Lovestedt Fleming
and
Russell P. Lovestedt.

Acknowledgements

With sincere gratitude to Meg Foard, who painstakingly formatted this book, and made many helpful suggestions about important details along the way.

With heartfelt thanks to my friends and family, who not only read my essays, but encouraged me to publish them.

Foreword

With a few exceptions, the essays included in this book appeared over a period of years as Other Voices opinion pieces in *The Union* newspaper, published in Grass Valley, California.

The essays are random in subject matter and varied in mood, a reflection of whatever came to the writer's mind at any given moment. Their only common thread is that they were written from the perspective of a widowed lady wending her way through her ninth decade during an era of breath-taking technological and social change.

The introductory very short essay appeared in the Sacramento Bee as a feature entitled, "I'm Just Saying----." The essay about my West Highland Terrier, Nessie, was published in *Bark* magazine, and the essay about the library appeared in a library anthology, *Open to All*, published by Comstock Bonanza Press, Grass Valley, California.

Birthdays
Accumulate,
The years accelerate,
Suddenly I find I'm doing
Eighty!

I Have This to Say About That

I have noticed that when you reach a certain age (80-plus!) people are apt to look at you in a startled way if you say something intelligent or even witty. You've been stereotyped as a befuddled old dear who is still unaccountably doddering about in public. At some social gatherings, you may be either totally ignored, or else fussed over by a patronizing altruist who feels duty bound to compliment you on being "alert."

Although I show signs of wear, I'm not a mental wreck, and I still have a few opinions I wish to express. So listen up!

Extending the Race

Due to good luck and considerable perseverance on my part, I have reached my eighty-fifth birthday, a respectable old age one might think. However, I am suddenly confronted with the disquieting news that, age-wise, "the 80's are now the new 60's." This arbitrary pronouncement has appeared in several newspaper and magazine articles I have read lately. My theory is that it was initiated by a committee of young, publicity-seeking gerontologists who looked at actuarial tables and concluded that, since the national trend is now toward a longer life-expectancy, it is acceptable to lop twenty years off a person's documented age. These are the same kind of people who will announce with false joviality that some frail centenarian is "100-years young." How patronizing! How deceitful!

This tinkering, this re-adjustment of one's life-time cannot be compared to daylight savings time when we either spring forward or fall back an hour. (And goodness knows that's bothersome enough.) *This* revision is much more drastic. We are talking in terms of a score of years, or two *decades*! I feel as if I've panted toward the finish line of a grueling marathon, only to have loud-speakers announce that the race has been extended by an additional twenty miles.

Lest you suppose that because I state that I am an old lady, I am weary of life and am preparing for imminent departure, I want to assure you that my intent is to live as long as I possibly can while still retaining my wits. I eat my fruit and veggies, practice tai chi and do the New York Times crossword puzzle every day. Despite this regimen, which ought to meet with AARP's approval, I acknowledge that some slippage has occurred. There is a wide difference between being a sprightly sixty-five and being a "well-preserved" eighty five. My synaptic responses have become more leisurely, my auditory acuity has diminished, there is often a significant delay in my reflexes, my balance is not always reliable, and my joints do not move with the smooth fluidity they once did. Therefore, I am unnerved by the prospect of being expected to operate with the same vigor and efficiency I did twenty years ago.

There has been comfort for me in the sunset years when I have felt entitled to smell the roses while somebody else pulled the weeds. I have had no misgivings about resting on the few laurels I accumulated. Monthly social security checks have brought joy. I utilize senior citizen discounts. *Now* it is being made to appear that I have received these benefits fraudulently. According to the new-age math, I was actually twenty years premature in my retirement and therefore not exactly eligible for social security or any of the other above-mentioned goodies. That is why I cannot accept this statistical "bonus" of two extra decades with any pretense of gratitude.

Also, in addition to my mundane worries about global warming and the head-long decline of civilization, I am presently subjected to the frightful anxiety of waiting until Social Security seizes upon this new "eighties are now the sixties" nonsense as a basis for a sweeping revision of their policies. Who knows if they may decide to demand immediate restitution, with interest, of all funds that have been paid to me. This will likely be accompanied by a statement in bold print listing the severe penalties to ensue if there is any lack of compliance, because, for sheer menace, there is nothing to be compared to a government agency in quest of one's last dollar.

I am prepared to fight with every means at my disposal against the summary appropriation of twenty of my birthdays. Furthermore, I am not eighty- five years *young*. I am eighty-five years *old* and that's the way I want to keep it. Who would *ever* have anticipated having to do battle for the right to be old!

Purchasing Power

Since I have crossed the threshold of my ninth decade, I have begun to carry a kind of mental actuarial table with me when I go shopping. When I'm considering any major purchase, this table automatically causes me to question, "Are you really going to live long enough to justify this kind of expenditure?"

This is not as morbid as it may sound. What is happening is that my practical side, developed as a child of the Depression when every penny was weighed at least twice before being spent, is manifesting itself.

It also bears upon the always present guilt question of whether I'm squandering my children's inheritance, and the more worrisome question of do I have enough money to last me for the rest of my life without becoming a burden to my aforementioned children?

My daughter and son show no signs of greed, and they consistently urge me to "Go for it, Mom," but I worry anyway, because it's my duty.

Considering all this, if I decide for sound economic reasons, to replace my old electric range, which has required several visits by technicians and two expensive replacement of parts, all costing more than doctors' house calls and major surgeries used to, then I'm confronted with another dilemma. Do I buy the top of the line, with its virtual lifetime guarantee, or do I settle for the cheaper utility model with a one-year warranty? I have to ponder whether my dear departed mother's advice to "always buy the very best you can afford---it always wears better"---is applicable in this situation.

Candidly speaking, I notice the ice is thinning underfoot. There has been decimation among the ranks of my friends and acquaintances, and I realize that life is more and more a day-to-day proposition. But, on the other hand, although my mirror image has quite a few spots and wrinkles, I was given high marks at my last physical examination six months ago---"for a woman your age."

I fantasize having my picture in the paper someday with a headline: "Centenarian Still Producing Gourmet Meals." I will, of course, be standing in front of the deluxe model stove, which has served so well over the years. Perhaps a lifetime warranty is warranted, so to speak.

Furthermore, I also suddenly remember reading somewhere that the late J. Paul Getty's advice about buying real estate was to purchase the best piece of property one could possibly afford in the absolutely best neighborhood. I realize that electric ranges and real estate are two different things, and that I'm in apples-versus-oranges territory, but quality and long-term return on investment are what we're discussing here. My mother and J. Paul Getty both had the kind of financial acumen one must respect.

The personable young salesman in the appliance store has no possible way of understanding that the white-haired lady, who is squinting at the price tags on each and every range in the showroom, is simultaneously waging an inner moral and philosophical battle, while bravely trying to look mortality in the eye.

He gives no indication of thinking of me as an indecisive ditherer. He is the soul of patience and good humor as he demonstrates the features of each range. He shrewdly deduces that the one with the electronic display panel, comparable to the instrument panel of a large commercial airliner, is not suitable for this particular customer.

With the air of a solicitous grandson, he confides that the model with Greatly Reduced for Quick Clearance sticker on it is really "just a piece of junk" He politely hustles me past it to the sleek, elegantly simple, high end model across the aisle.

Of course, you know what happens.

"I'm sure you'll be happy you bought this range," the young salesman says. "It will give you many years of fine service." I am thinking it had jolly- well better last 20 years to fit in with my plans for my centennial picture in the paper.

"It always pays to buy quality," the young salesman says approvingly. He seems to be exactly in tune with my mother and J. Paul Getty. He should go far.

Enjoying The Sunset

There are a lot of things about growing old that nobody ever prepares us for. Perhaps this is just as well, because we might want to forgo the experience altogether. For example, I had no idea my hair would grow thin. I have never been bushy-haired, but until I reached eighty, I had no worries about my scalp being adequately covered. It now requires some adroit combing on the part of my hairdresser and me, to keep little patches of pink from showing through my gray locks. This has caused me to develop a sympathetic feeling for such an unlikely person as Donald Trump. I am sure his hair-style is meant to camouflage his receding hair-line. Bizarre is better than bare, maybe.

I had every intention of aging gracefully, but from just a purely physical standpoint, this is not feasible. Alas, even rising from a chair with an easy fluid motion is impossible to do when one's knees have locked in a sitting position. The best one can hope for is to be able to push oneself upright without groaning. A positive-thinking friend of mine is of the opinion that giving voice to discomfort only serves to exacerbate the problem. .Therefore, as Archie Bunker would have said, I "stifle myself." I keep quiet about any twinges I feel. However, there is nothing I can do about the popping sounds my joints make.

Once standing, the challenge is to keep from staggering or lurching about and bumping into things. I have become unbalanced. My equilibrium is something I once took for granted. Now, if I bend over suddenly, instead of stooping, (trying to spare my knees, you know) my body tends to want to flop further forward, like a weighted doll. So far, I haven't fallen on my face, thank goodness, but I am learning to bend over slowly and cautiously.

Then there is the matter of scrabbling. My organizational skills have evidently deteriorated, because I find it increasingly difficult to locate things in my purse. I tend to paw through the contents searching for my grocery list, or car keys or spare hankie. This is unsettling to my daughter who remembers that a dear, but dotty, relative was forever rummaging distractedly through her purse or coat pockets for lost items and would sometimes haul everything out onto the nearest

7

flat surface, the better to sort through it. For my daughter's sake, I am making a serious effort not to scrabble.

A friend with excellent posture sometimes briskly reminds me to "stand up straight." She has even given me a recipe for how to do this: "Stand with your hands at your sides, then turn you hands palm forward and stick out your thumbs." This works. I become a ramrod. So now when I walk my dog, Nessie, I hook her leash around my arm and stride forth, palms out, thumbs extended. I am then perceived as a peculiar, but erect, old lady taking her exercise. Fortunately Nessie, a West Highland Terrier, is a very accepting kind of dog who doesn't seem to mind appearing in public with me, no matter what I do.

I have composed a kind of mantra for myself: Don't groan, don't scrabble, don't slouch.

Now at the end of the day, wearied by all the conscious effort it seems to require just to function and to maintain a presentable appearance, I relax on my deck with a glass of iced tea. I look out over my garden, which is exuberant with spring flowers. I think of my family, especially my son and daughter, who I not only love, but like very much. I consider the steadfast kindness of my friends and remember my adventure-filled life with a wonderful man. Suddenly, I feel I am almost floating. I am dazzled by the pure splendor of life itself. What a gift! I want to fall to my knees, creaky as they are, and, like Shakespeare's lark, "sing hymns at heaven's gate."

Old age may not be graceful, I think to myself, but it is a time of grace. How marvelous it is to live in the present and be able to cherish what is past. Memory has softened sorrow and distilled joy. Colors are more vivid, the scent of honeysuckle is sweeter, love is easier to express, and more gratefully accepted. Poetry speaks with a clearer voice. The sunset hour is particularly beautiful.

The Realm of Unlimited Possibilities

Sometimes I arrive at the library a few minutes before it opens. Almost always there are other people waiting on the steps, and there is an immediate sense of fellowship amongst us, as if we might be prepared to give each other a secret handshake. We are an eager and expectant small group waiting for the closed sign on the door to be reversed, listening for the little click that announces the door is now unlocked. Because I am old, I am often deferred to, urged to go in first, but no matter what the order, each of us courteously holds the door open for the person behind us. We are imbued with the kind of civility appropriate to a company of adventure- seekers about to enter a realm of unlimited possibilities.

Invariably, I stop first at the shelves of new non-fiction books. When looking at the array of volumes dealing with the real world, I immediately begin to have a surreal experience. There is no way for my brain to accommodate in any conventional way the subject matter that ranges from how to raise a puppy or get a divorce or make wise investments, to how to read tarot cards and/or travel in outer space. My selections are mostly random, and may deal with matters that have held no previous interest for me. These serendipitous choices have amazed, horrified, delighted, flabbergasted and educated me. I am rarely disappointed.

Next, I browse in the new fiction section, seeking a best-seller recommended by a friend. I consider eye-catching titles, examine dust jacket illustrations, check the reviewer comments, read brief author bios, and eyeball the author's picture. With the same kind of discrimination as a candy-lover picking his favorite caramels out of a box of chocolates, I make my selection and drop another couple of volumes into my book bag.

Then I remember that the reason I came to the library in the first place was to locate a copy of Don Marquis' The Adventures of Archie and Mehitebel, published in 1925. This is one of the choices my reading group has made. When I cannot find it among the M's on the fiction shelves, the librarian locates it for me in the literature section. We laugh together as we look at the illustration on the cover of the old volume, and she comments that it has been years since she's thought about that particular book. She obligingly scans the computer to see if the County Library system has any other holdings by the same author. My book bag now bulges with as heavy a load as I can carry.

While my books are being processed, I look about me and am surprised to see that now there are many more of us in the library than the flock of early birds I came in with. All of the computers are busy, their users staring into them with the hunched fixity of the technologically involved. A man and woman are discussing possible selections from the video section. A lone man is looking over the collection of audio books. Several people are seated at the reading tables with outspread newspapers or stacks of magazines. A woman is gathering up pages from a copying machine.

I realize that I am standing in the midst of marvels. I am amazed by the bustle and vigor of this library, so seemingly unrelated to my home town's small Carnegie library, the one I first entered eighty years ago. That was a hushed and hallowed place which I humbly loved, a place where I tip-toed up to the librarian's desk to check out the Raggeddy Ann books I adored. Going to the library was not too different from going to church, and indeed I did learn to worship there: I developed a lifelong reverence for books.

The library of my old age is a lively place which I enter without my childhood humility but still with the joyful anticipation of long ago. The old reverence lingers, too, and I carry away my bag full of books with a feeling of exaltation.

Adapt or Perish

If technological advances had been left up to me, we might still be living in caves and digging our dinner out from under rocks with a pointed stick. When it comes to change, I am never on the cutting edge.

Fortunately, however, progress has always been in more innovative hands than mine. By the time I arrived on the scene in 1921, many civilized amenities were already in place. I grew up in Cheyenne, Wyoming, where we lived in a snug brick house and the groceries were delivered to our back porch from the corner grocery store. The inventions my parents marveled over and took pride in possessing, the electric stove and washing machine, the victrola, the crystal radio, the vacuum cleaner, the telephone with the voice that said "Number Please," were simply part of my surroundings. I took these conveniences for granted and used them adeptly, just as today's children nonchalantly handle, computers, VCR's and DVD's.

The technology we are born into is usually not a problem for us. It's the innovations that are introduced later in life that cause the difficulties. I can remember my German grandfather being absolutely terrified of the telephone. This was the courageous man, mind you, who sailed from Europe to the United States with a pregnant wife, three small daughters and an infant son, to homestead in Nebraska. "By gollies, I don't touch dot t'ing!" he declared when urged to talk into it to speak to his daughter in Omaha. I undoubtedly smiled in a superior way at the time, just as my grand-children covertly smiled at each other when I vowed that I would never touch a computer.

Well, Grandpa learned to use the telephone, although he always bellowed into it, firm in his belief that vocal transmission depended solely on his lung power. And I am learning to use a computer, haltingly, prayerfully, always with an incomplete understanding of what I am doing. Both Grandpa and I reluctantly bowed to the law of survival: Adapt or perish.

I have to tell you, though, that adapting does not preclude looking back on olden time with a certain amount of wistfulness.

11

Am I about to say those were the good old days? Well, yes, I am--- in a way. Would I like to go back to them? Well, no, I wouldn't---not exactly.

What I actually want to do is stop the fast-forward button somebody has pressed. Our time-saving devices seem to have robbed us of the time for the personal touch in the transactions of daily life, for the leisurely face to face encounters that encourage the building of understanding and friendship. For me, these things are humanly necessary. I still like the idea of a live voice saying "Number Please." That's why, when I call a business or agency, I always wait through a long menu for the option of last resort---the button to push that connects me with a real person.

I realize that resisting the new and clinging to the old is considered a hallmark of old age. Yet sometimes we need to look at the cost of progress in terms of the impact it has on the quality of our life and consider how much we are controlling technology and how much technology is controlling us.

When my computer was "down" for a couple of days last month, I suddenly realized I was "up." Why? I was released from the compulsion to check my e-mail and sort through the junk messages, to browse the internet, to slip in a few games of solitaire, to struggle again with my newly installed Word program. I recognized that I spend a lot of time every day peering into Windows instead of looking out of windows. My world had changed from round to flat---as flat as a computer screen. But do I want to part with my computer? I do not. It is a marvelous, magical tool and I cannot imagine life without it.

So how do we strike a balance? I'll tell you what---e-mail me when you have a free afternoon. We'll have a cup of tea together in my garden. I'd so love to see you again to find out what's been happening in your life. And I'd like to see the expression on your face when I tell you what's happening in mine. Please don't bring your cell phone.

Here's To Your Health

It stands to reason that by the time you have lived far longer than you ever expected to, you may have had to undergo some overhaul and repair, not to mention a replacement of parts. And you're going to have some cherished contemporaries who have an assortment of things wrong with them. At this time of life I notice we inquire after each other's health somewhat diffidently.

"Um, you're looking fine, are you feeling okay?"

Last week when a friend who has been dealing with a series of health problems called from Southern California, I nerved myself to inquire how she was doing.

"Well, I'm seeing every kind of doctor but an obstetrician," she replied with a laugh. Then she went on to tell me about a long trip she is planning to take next month with a favorite travel partner, and after that described the wonderful cruise they enjoyed last spring. Apparently during the intervals she spends at home, she allots whatever she considers a reasonable amount of time for various specialists to do their probing and testing and then away she goes again to have a good time.

For many years I have carried on an alternate-month correspondence with a Cheyenne high school classmate who lives in Laramie, Wyoming. We have not seen each other since 1940. Of course we both know that we are "little old ladies," but I still picture her as "Miss Frontier," the queen of Cheyenne's famous Frontier Days rodeo, and I suppose I still appear on her mind's eye as young and reasonably fair. There is something to be said for this kind of relationship.

One of Oscar Wilde's witticisms was that "The tragedy of old age is not that one is old but that one is young." This is the paradox of aging: Outward appearances often belie how one feels on the inside.

When my friend and I write to each other we discuss our feelings about everything from arthritis to widowhood to retirement homes, acknowledging that these are facts of life for us, but any melancholy is removed because we are, after all, still young girls together.

13

We go on to speak of books and family and all the things that make us happy. I describe my garden and give her the details of my grandson's wedding. She tells me of cross-country skiing with a group of seniors and admits she feels silly and kind of guilty over having recently purchased a small SUV. I tell her I hope the SUV is a red one.

The Southern California friend I mentioned earlier once told me, "I don't mind getting old, but I do mind getting ugly! Just look at all these lines and age spots!" I was taken by surprise, because I consider her very attractive and I was privately marveling at her vitality and intelligence. I took her age spots for granted just as I accept my own most of the time.

However, sometimes one is jolted into awareness of the ravages of time by such things as the unblinking stare of a great-grandchild who remarks, "You're awfully old, aren't you Grandma?" Or the over-solicitous young hostess who does everything but follow you about with a wheel chair in case you might be going to have a sinking spell. There is no way to explain in these circumstances that although you appear rickety, desiccated and pre-historic, and may actually at that very moment be experiencing mild indigestion plus a certain amount of chronic joint pain, you are still enjoying life immensely and are terribly pleased to be around. There is no point, either, in quoting Oscar Wilde.

It is true that many old people are prepared to respond with a detailed inventory of body parts when someone asks how they feel. They are like the old gentleman who, when asked how he was, replied, "Well, my head aches, my elbow is stiff, my back is sore and my feet hurt. And to tell you the truth, *I* don't feel so good either." There is a temptation to dwell upon a long list of fascinating infirmities and to compare scars. The complaints are legitimate. On the other hand, it is equally true that when some elderly persons with multiple health problems say "I feel fine!" they are speaking honestly, too. Their reply is from that contradictory inner self that dismisses outward appearances. They are still welcoming life's possibilities, no matter how limited they may be. Quite often there is a smile, and even a hint of mischief, in their eyes.

The Touch of Your Hand

The most alarming news I have heard lately, was reported in what was intended to be an up-beat feature on the evening newscast. The bright young anchor woman announced that a group of scientists is working on a plan to employ robots to provide in-home care for the elderly. I immediately experienced tachycardia and the frisson of terror I always feel when confronted with the possibility of yet another complex system designed to simplify life.

The "Look what technology can do for us now!" film clips were not reassuring. They showed a kindly old couple who wished to spend their remaining years in the home they loved. They had agreed to have their daily activities monitored while they tried out the electronic gadgetry that science proposed as a means to by-pass institutional care.

Accordingly, their every move was followed by equipment probably akin to a fish-finder or some other kind of peeping Tom. Although bathroom activities were not shown on television, one must surely assume that anything of that importance was meticulously recorded and dispassionately evaluated at some distant control center. A helpful device located the man's misplaced eyeglasses and an image on a computer screen showed him their location. Then a disembodied voice with overtones of faux-warmth congratulated him, "You have found your glasses." (Positive reinforcement, you see, for the person being programmed to respond like a robot.) Then the woman was informed it was time to take her ten o'clock pill. Later on, the disembodied voice, with a note of faux-concern, inquired, "Is the headache you had when we talked to you at ten o'clock better now?" I am not certain whether the woman responded verbally into the empty air, pressed a yes/no button, or made plans to sue for scientific harassment. The couple had a bewildered, hunted look.

Speaking as an "older person" who has made an uneasy accommodation to computer technology, I can tell you I will resist to my last breath being ordered around by it during my declining years, even if it is tricked out as a cute little robotic helper. Anything purporting to be your willing slave is inherently dangerous. As any slave-holder of your acquaintance will tell you, slaves require constant attention and maintenance, meaning that eventually slaves actually enslave their masters. Pushcart Press has published a book, *Minutes of the Lead Pencil Club,* which is dedicated to "Pulling the plug on the electronic revolution." The major concern the book expresses is "about the influence of computers and assorted electronic inventions on our lives." This is precisely what scares me, too.

My computer has a coy little pop-up that asks, "Do you want to stay connected?" Well, goodness, yes, I want to stay connected--- humanly connected, that is. But that is exactly the connection our technology is destroying. Government, professions, businesses and even the so-called "help lines," have electronically walled themselves off from direct human contact. When we call any of them for information or, perish the thought, assistance, we are obliged to listen to more disembodied voices than Joan of Arc ever dreamt of, some with heavy accents and from places as far away as New Delhi, India. I never feel more helpless or isolated than when I am groping my way through a long "menu" that has no item exactly pertinent to my need. I am astonished if I chance to receive a direct answer to a simple question.

We talk about using e-mail "to keep in touch," ignoring the fact that the operant word is "touch." For example, much of what we receive as e-mail lacks anything resembling the personal touch, and is, in fact, reprinted lists of jokes or aphorisms the sender is using to tell us he has at least thought about us. He is sharing with us in a way, but he has taken a short-cut by not giving us access to his own thoughts and feelings, thereby excluding us, leaving us somehow disappointed.

Our basic need for the warmth of human contact cannot be met by technology. If, or when, I enter the "assisted living" phase of life, I want a sentient, breathing, possibly eccentric, certainly fallible, but above all, compassionate, human being nearby. I refuse to consider holding hands with a robot. I do not want automated or virtual care. I want the real thing!

Identity Crisis

As I have grown older, I have become the victim of a subtle kind of identity theft. I am constantly being told I look like somebody else. Whenever I am introduced to anyone, I have come to expect some version of this scenario: "Hmmm, I feel as if I've met you before." This is followed by a puzzled scrutiny, after which they will exclaim triumphantly, "I know what it is---you look so much like Aunt Mary!" If there is another person around who also knows Aunt Mary, they will call that person over for corroboration.

"Who does she remind you of?" they will ask with the superior smile of one who has just solved a difficult riddle and now wants to test other people's intelligence. This is a tense moment for me and for the verifying party. They're eager to give the right answer and I am in fear of their responding with the name of one of our least attractive public figures. Occasionally there is agreement that I do look a bit like Aunt Mary, although of course Aunt Mary's nose is smaller. They assure me that Aunt Mary is a wonderful woman.

The effect of these comparisons is to make me feel like a fashion knockoff, or like the generic substitute for a costlier prescription. Perhaps I'm being over-sensitive because people mean well and expect me to be complimented by their connecting me to someone they know, never mind who it is.

Recently in my dentist's waiting room, a white-haired fellow sitting near me, fished a picture out of his wallet. "I want you to take a good look at this," he said, with tears in his eyes. "I guess I've been staring at you, but you're so like my wife who died last year." The lady in the snapshot was no beauty, but I murmured ambiguously, "How nice." I could tell it made him feel better, but I can't say it cheered me up at all.

Last week I was stopped by the highway patrol. I had allowed my car to drift too close to the center line of the highway. "Were you talking on a cell phone?" the officer asked. When I explained that it was a lapse of attention on my part, and that I don't own a cell phone, he said briskly, "Please keep your eye on the road and drive safely. We wouldn't want anything to happen to you---you look so much like my mother." Under the circumstances it was certainly better to look like his mother than an escaped felon.

On one memorable occasion I was standing at the meat market counter, absorbed in my contemplation of the pork chops, when I was grabbed from behind in a huge bear-hug. When I twisted around to see who was holding me, a very flustered gentleman exclaimed, "Oh, I do beg your pardon! From the back you're a dead ringer for Dorothy!" Evidently I am familiar from almost any angle. It was not such a bad experience, though. His cologne was nice.

So yes, it's true, not all my adventures as a look-alike have been uniformly bleak. Actually a positive experience occurred when I was on vacation in Banff. While in the serving line for the buffet brunch in the hotel dining room, I felt myself receiving the familiar once-over from the man next to me.

"Excuse me," he said, "I suppose you get tired of people telling you how much you resemble the late Ethel Barrymore. But I just have to tell you, too. She was a dear friend of mine."

"What a lovely thing to hear!" I said fervently He could have no idea *how* lovely it was. When I was young, I fantasized being told I looked like Ingrid Bergman or Lauren Bacall, but it never happened. Now, here I was, late in life, being likened to Ethel Barrymore!

For a while after that, I gazed at myself in the mirror with improved self-esteem. Sometimes Ethel Barrymore's distinguished countenance seemed super-imposed upon mine.

Then I had cataract surgery. My first good look at myself following the operation was all but heart-stopping. I saw with perfect clarity all the wrinkles and age spots which had heretofore been mercifully blurred. Good heavens! I did not look like myself at all! I looked like someone else entirely.

Unfortunately it wasn't Ethel Barrymore.

Apprenticeship for Marriage

Prior to my marriage in 1942, my mother had spent years preparing me to someday become a proper wife. She taught me how to darn socks and turn the frayed collar on a shirt. I learned how to splice the good material salvaged from worn sheets so that double sheets became twin bed sheets.

I was trained to sort the laundry into lights and darks and pre-soak the most soiled items over-night. I understood the importance of using bluing on white goods and I could prepare starch of exactly the right consistency for the dress shirts the men in my family wore. Furthermore, I could iron one of these shirts in about fifteen minutes. Speed mattered since we had fifteen or twenty shirts to iron every week. (Our German neighbor could iron a shirt in twelve minutes, but then she had the advantage of having worked in a laundry, so she was actually a professional whereas I was merely a gifted amateur.) I memorized two immutable laws of housekeeping: (1) Dusting is something you do often, whether you want to or not, and this includes the lowest rungs on chairs and the curlicue legs of Jacobean style furniture, and (2) no bed should remain unmade past 8:30 a.m.

From age five, I helped my mother in the kitchen. This I loved to do. One of my first jobs was to remove the string from the parcels from the butcher shop and wind it around an ever enlarging ball of string we kept in a kitchen drawer. I was eventually promoted to folding wax paper, saved from bread wrappers, into neat squares so that they could be re-used to wrap sandwiches for school lunches. Later I cut out cookies, spacing them carefully so that the rolled-out dough was used most efficiently, and I learned to slice noodles into thin, even strips. I was allowed to brag about these accomplishments at the dinner table.

Because my mother started her marriage with few cooking skills, she was determined that I be competent at baking and canning and preparing meals and be spared the stress of her on-the-job learning experience. It was important to her that food not only taste good but also look attractive and be presented on a neatly laid table with pretty china. We used cloth napkins and each of us had our own napkin ring.

When I culled my recipe files a while back, I found the recipes for my mother's spice cake, horseradish sauce, sugar cookies, chokecherry jelly, watermelon pickles and heavenly hash, along with her recipe for dog food (boiled beef heart, cornmeal and carrots), and also her recipes for a mustard plaster and home brew. The mustard plaster helped my grandfather survive a bout of pneumonia during one of Cheyenne's bitter winters, and the home brew provided what he needed to survive the rigors of Prohibition. My mother was a hard act to follow!

The truth is that I did not really follow in her footsteps. I settled in California with my new husband who worked in an aircraft factory, and during the first decade of our marriage, the American lifestyle underwent such rapid and drastic change due to World War II and the ensuing advances in technology and manufacturing that the old ways of doing things no longer applied. Along with the rest of the country we enjoyed post-war prosperity, and I therefore abandoned frugality and did not darn socks, turn shirt collars or splice sheets. I still sorted the laundry into lights and darks, but pre-soaked nothing, used no bluing and starched very few items. My lovely automatic washer and dryer took care of everything while I whizzed my new vacuum cleaner around the house cleaning and dusting every corner and crevice.

The one area where I did adhere closely to my mother's teaching was cooking. I continued to bake and cook everything from scratch and tried to present attractive meals. This came as a welcome surprise to my husband whose whirlwind courtship had not included any in-depth investigation of my culinary skills.

Before I left home, the final gift my mother placed in my hope chest, atop the embroidered tea-towels and hand-hemmed linens, was a book entitled *A Thousand Ways to Please a Husband.* This was not, as you might suppose, a sex manual. It was a cook book. There was one thing my mother thought it was up to me to figure out for myself.

Staying Power

My father once commented, "If you're thinking of marrying someone, you'd better be sure that's the face you want to see across the table from you for the rest of your life." At the time, I laughed, because I knew my father was merely reinforcing what I had been brought up to believe: Marriage was for keeps---not to "be entered into lightly or unadvisedly."

When I did marry, it was to a man who also meant it when he said "until death do us part." Then we discovered that marriage is a perpetual care enterprise, and we spent the next 53 years cultivating love and understanding.

Most of the families in the modest, suburban Southern California neighborhood where we settled in the 1940's, were conventional in the same way we were. Couples were married and intended to stay that way. We worked most week-ends on do-it-yourself projects to improve our homes, and had high hopes of raising polite and reasonable children. Male and female roles in this sheltered, comfortable enclave, remained pretty sharply defined, the pace of life was manageable. Our futures seemed predictable.

Despite this, in 1960, our national turmoil eventually impinged upon my consciousness. I read Betty Friedan's *The Feminine Mystique,* and although I did not feel any need to be "liberated," I realized I had some unfinished business. To my husband's alarm, I decided at mid-life to return to college to complete my education. I suddenly found myself among a throng of disaffected youth who spoke of the police as "pigs," stated that anyone over thirty could not be trusted, despised all big business corporations, and labeled my generation hypocritical. Unsmiling, stringy -haired girls in sack-like garments handed out flowers and urged others to "make love, not war," and Timothy Leary's advice was to "Turn on, tune in, and drop out." In sociology classes I was introduced to the concept of "serial monogamy" which was said to be permeating our society, and further learned that even people who were married remained in a state of "perpetual availability." Good lord! Talk about culture shock!

I was astounded but at the same time exhilarated. The civil rights movement became real to me. I listened to African Americans students speak out against discrimination and segregation. I understood for the first time why some young men had become draft dodgers. I saw Muhammed Ali stride across our university campus followed by an admiring crowd of students who honored him as a hero who had been true to his ideals at considerable cost to himself. I learned that gender bias was a reality, and that aspiring and capable women were denied access to certain careers and opportunities simply on the basis of their sex. Police helicopters hovered overhead, monitoring student demonstrations.

My foray into higher education was exactly what it was supposed to be---a true learning experience. I wouldn't have missed it for the world. And now we come to my however---

In social change, there is always an element of extremism, (who needed Timothy Leary!) and it then remains for us to sift through discarded values to see if there are some things we threw away too hastily. One thing I am suggesting we take another look at is the old style attitude toward marriage.

It is now trendy to speak of the "bonding process," but this is not to be confused with the "bonds of matrimony." Commitment appears to be synonymous with institutional incarceration. There is certainly freedom to enter into relationships, but these seem to be of the quick-disposal variety. The "serial monogamy" that worried me forty years ago has lately turned into a kind of limited time-share with an easy cancellation option.

Our emphasis on social and sexual equality seems to have destroyed our patience for the time-consuming, labor-intensive effort required to build enduring marriage. Common sense tells us that not every marriage is going to work. But what would happen if we once again emphasized permanence and dedication? What if we sought out "significant others" whose faces we wanted to see across the table from us for the rest of our lives? This is idealistic, of course, and romantic, too, but what's wrong with that! Why shouldn't we reach for the stars? Some faces become incredibly beautiful over time.

Woe Is Me

When, on the darkest days of our life, we need an understanding individual to whom to tell our troubles, the main problem is to find a suitable listener. I have found it all but impossible to locate a person who is willing to just listen and not interrupt my tale of utter disaster with a comment such as, "I know *exactly* what you're talking about---only the guy who backed into *my* new car didn't just make a dent, he mashed in the whole driver's side and rammed my car against a lamp post. I was trapped inside for half an hour and they had to use the 'jaws of life' to get me out. I was in the hospital for three weeks. Of course the car was totaled and I hadn't gotten around to having it insured."

The last thing we want to hear about when we are in extremis, is somebody else's relatively picayune problems. It is essential to establish that *we* are the most miserable one around. We are the main attraction and will not abide competition. Above all, we don't want a session of "Can You Top This." We are so absolutely wretched we want it understood that our troubles are not only monumental, they are incomparable, beyond the realm of known human experience. Our difficulties make the Slough of Despond in Pilgrim's Progress seem like a mud puddle.

And certainly in this dreadful hour of our life, we do not want some robust, sanguine type who is so relentlessly optimistic he would look upon the apocalypse as a kind of block party. This sort listens in a cursory way and then callously suggests that "tomorrow will be a brighter day." This is accompanied by a pat on the shoulder and the additional patronizing reassurance that "this too shall pass." Hah! The immensity of our suffering does not register with such a person. Anyone with true sensitivity would gasp in horror at our description of what we are going through and exclaim, "I have never before in my life heard of anything so dreadful! I can't imagine how you are managing to remain upright!"

Above all, we do not want some glib type who assumes that all problems are amenable to solution. Any listener who slips in a sentence beginning, "If I were you, I'd get on the internet and check…" has missed the point entirely. *Our* problems defy remedy. There *is* no way out. We are doomed and all we ask is that somebody listens to our final words as the curtain descends upon the last act of our tragic existence. We want a friend like the one Socrates had who will accept that hemlock is indeed the beverage *de jour* and is prepared to chronicle our sufferings for posterity.

When we are sitting in sack-cloth and ashes and weeping and wailing and gnashing our teeth, and otherwise lamenting in true biblical style, it is necessary to have an appalled witness who is up to doing a little empathetic forehead smiting, too. (Unfortunately having a corps of professional mourners does not seem to have caught on in Western society as it has in other parts of the world, because they would be exactly appropriate to the occasion.) There is absolutely nothing to be said for suffering in silence or, worse yet, in solitude.

H-m-m-m, you know, as I've been talking to you, it occurs to me that I've always considered *you* quite a sensitive person who has the capacity to tune into other people's feelings. Let me tell you what happened to me while I was on my way over here to see you…….

Teachers

Occasionally I have a nightmare in which I am in a class room full of children I am supposed to teach, but I have not the least idea how to do it. The children look at me expectantly until it dawns on them that I am a fraud. They immediately turn into shrieking, taunting imps who dismantle the room. I cannot regain control. I am certain the principal is lurking in the corridor and will soon charge through the door, loudly berating me for my incompetence. I am terrified of both the children and the principal. This is the moment at which my pounding heart awakens me. I fervently thank heaven for my return to reality.

When I mentioned this dream to a friend of mine who is a retired teacher, she smiled ruefully. "I experienced almost that situation in real life. After my first day in a classroom, I was so demoralized I went home and flung myself on my bed sobbing, 'I just can't do this! I don't know how'!" Nevertheless, she did summon the courage to go on, perhaps because she had no other choice. She continued to teach for thirty years. As she described her career to me, it was evident she remembered the years with joy. Her eyes sparkled when she talked about some of her long ago pupils ---the bright, the hungry, the dreamy, and the ornery ones and the little fellow who was so shy she had to hold his hand to make him feel secure enough to learn anything.

My late sister-in-law also enjoyed a long and outstanding career as an elementary school teacher. Because of her teaching skills, parents clamored to have their children placed in her fifth grade class, and of course, like most strong teachers, she was often given many of the difficult children, the disruptive ones from the lower grades whose sinister reputations preceded them.

"What on earth do you do?" I once asked when I knew she was starting the school year with a particularly challenging class. "Do you smile a lot and try to make friends with the tough ones?"

"Good heavens, no! I don't smile at all. It's not up to me to please my students--- it's up to them to please me by doing what they're in school to do. The first thing I impress on my students is that school is their job. There are standards they must meet. They have a responsibility to get their work done and treat others respectfully. When they begin to meet those expectations, then is when I begin to smile. With the class I have this year, I probably won't smile until sometime in November." One of her classes, twenty years after they had passed through her classroom, organized a reunion to thank her for the contribution she had made to their lives.

As I think back eight decades to my own school days, I feel a certain pride in being able to name every one of my grade school teachers. However if one considers that a child spends approximately six hours of every week day under a teacher's supervision, it stands to reason that teachers should be as firmly planted in one's memory as family members are. Even now, the shadow of my sixth grade teacher, austere Miss Hingston, falls over me if I merely toy with the idea of dodging some commitment.

Along with rigorous academic preparation for junior high school, she also included character building. In order to strengthen our moral fiber, she insisted we memorize noble phrases from Shakespeare: "Who steals my purse steals trash, but he who filches from me my good name robs me of that which ne'er enriches him but leaves me poor indeed." And "Sweet are the uses of adversity, which like the toad, ugly and venomous, yet has a jewel in the middle of his forehead." There were maxims, too: "Words unspoken sometimes fall back dead, but God himself cannot kill them when they're said." And admonitions: "Lost yesterday, two golden hours, each set with sixty diamond minutes. No reward is offered, for they are lost and gone forever."

My long-ago teachers have been dead for many years, but unlike General MacArthur's old soldiers, they have not faded away. They enjoy a certain kind of immortality in my mind. I marvel hat they were brave enough to teach.

What's The Word?

Seventy-five years ago I was eliminated from the Wyoming state spelling bee when I misspelled "chrysanthemum." This of course was a major disappointment to me. I had studied page after page of words for the event and had also consulted with a previous winner for advice. I longed to emulate the success of this brainy, but arrogant girl, who snickered at typographical errors in books and magazines and sniffed at people who fiddled with a legitimate word like "night," which, she pointed out, appeared as "nite" on the marquee of our local movie theater: "Friday Bank Nite. Be present to win $200 dollars." I'm certain her reaction to today's text-messaging would be apoplectic.

Then, twenty years ago, my grandson reached the regional finals of the California state spelling bee. I thought perhaps redemption was at hand. One of our family members might yet succeed where I had failed. But no, this was not to be. He faltered on the word, "hennin."

"What in the world is a hennin?" I asked his mother. My daughter had once taken a course in costume design so she knew that "a hennin is a tall, conical or heart-shaped hat sometimes worn with a flowing veil." I think it's what medieval ladies used to wear when they dressed up to attend a joust.

This reminded me of our family's "word of the day" program, instituted by my husband when our children were growing up. We took turns posting in our breakfast nook, unusual words we had either heard or run across in our reading. The idea was to enlarge our vocabularies with new and interesting words which we could use in general conversation. One of the rules was that the word should not be so obscure that other people wouldn't know what we were talking about. "Hennin" would never have qualified for our breakfast nook.

Given my interest in words, you will understand why I was delighted by the popular 2006 movie "Akeelah and the Bee." In case you missed it, it is the story of how an inner city child, with no family encouragement whatever, is relentlessly coached by a stern tutor (almost like our young Olympic gymnasts!) to winning the national spelling bee in Washington D.C. The contest, as portrayed, was as much of a white-knuckler as any sporting competition.

Research on the internet informs me that the national spelling bee has been in existence since 1925.This annual event has been sponsored by Scripps since 1941, with a three-year hiatus during World War II. Originally there were only nine contestants as compared to more than three hundred today. Under Disney sponsorship, the contest has been shown on public television and the final stages have aired on the ABC network since 1994.

It is interesting to look at the words the early winners spelled and compare them to the winning words of recent contestants. In 1925 the winning word was "gladiolus." (That's a lot easier than chrysanthemum, don't you think?) Through the thirties and up until the sixties the contest words at least looked like words we might have encountered before. After that such words as xanthosis, vivisepulture, autochthonous, ursprache and serrifine, to name a few, were winning words. These are specialist's words, I suppose, and are of such low utility value for daily discourse that I suspect none of us will ever hear them uttered in conversation.

And speaking of the unusual, I remember how astounded I was when my brother came home from junior high school long ago with the information that "antidisestablishmentarianism" (28 letters) was the longest English word in the dictionary. Unfortunately he did not live long enough to marvel with me at the word ""floccinaucinihilipilification" (29 letters), which I discovered by chance in my unabridged dictionary last year. I have never been the same since!

"Supercalifragilisticexpialidocious" from "Mary Poppins" is also in that dictionary but is listed as a nonsense word specifically created to be the longest word in the dictionary, so its bona fides are questionable to say the least!

Words are delightful and tricky things, and, as was so often the case, Mark Twain was precisely on target when he remarked, "The difference between the right word and the almost right word is the difference between lightning and a lightning bug." The same thing is true of spelling. Almost right won't do.

Fame by Association

At eight years of age, I discovered that if you yourself are not famous, the next best thing is to have some connection with a person who is. One of my older brothers was hit by a Model-A Ford as he was crossing the street, and, at school, I became known as "the sister of the kid who got run over." This kind of notoriety was a heady experience for a third-grader with no major, or even minor, achievements to brag about. But I recognized an opportunity when I saw it. I summoned all my capabilities for the dramatic to capitalize on my brother's misfortune.

"Yes," I said somberly, "all three of the bones in his right leg are broken. He had a compound fracture. He's still in shock." I was quoting verbatim my mother's telephone conversation with her sister in Denver. "What's a compound fracture?"

I had asked the same question myself, but now I acted as if this were the sort of thing any well-informed person ought to know. With an air of condescension I explained, "It's when broken bones stick out through your skin---one of my brother's bones was sticking clear out of his pant leg."

There was a collective gasp. I savored the incomparable satisfaction of being the focus of a ring of appalled faces. My classmates were aghast and agog.

The main problem with sensationalism, however, is that it dissipates quickly if not replenished with new and juicy tidbits. I was able to maintain my position of vicarious celebrity for about a week by issuing daily bulletins of a quasi medical nature. First, I described the trapeze placed over my brother's bed to help him shift positions a little. To hear me tell it, he was performing incredible acrobatic feats on some complex mechanism. I drew a picture of his leg in a foot-to-hip plaster cast in an impossibly elevated position with an enormous weight dangling from it.

Then I talked about the young cowpuncher in the room across the hall from my brother. "He fell off his horse and he's in a coma. He hasn't come to for six weeks. His head's all bandaged up. I can see right into his room and watch him breathe."

29

After that I announced I had counted three doors at our small hospital with "No Visitors" signs. "That means the people are probably dying." I explained callously.

Finally, digging really deep, I mentioned the guinea pigs in the hospital basement. "They keep them there for experiments. They give them germs to eat and then wait to see how sick they get and if they're going to die."

After that, I was out of ideas. (My brother recovered without a limp and lived another sixty-five years.)

What triggered the foregoing memories was a recent trip to the super-market. I was in a slow-moving line and all of us in the queue had time to study the lurid covers on the display of tabloids. The man standing behind me was outraged by what he saw.

"Who in the world thinks up all this wild stuff!" he exclaimed to his wife.

"Oh, probably a group of cynical types have a conference and try to decide what's the most outlandish thing they can publish about some celebrity without being sued," she replied.

"Well, if I was Prince Charles, I'd sure sue somebody over that picture," he said, pointing to a maximally unflattering photo of the prince with Camilla. "They look like an ad for people with acute allergies."

"And, look here! You're not even safe when you're dead! They keep resurrecting Jackie Onassis and the Kennedys and even poor little Jon-Benet Ramsey – wouldn't you think they could let them rest in peace!"

"People always want a connection to the rich and famous, dead or alive," his wife responded.

"I'd say the people who print this stuff have got to be pretty hard-up for material!"

The man had put his finger precisely on the problem I encountered decades ago. Even if your original material is good, it has to be constantly augmented and judiciously embellished to hold public interest. Eventually, no matter what you do, the subject matter grows thin. I could have told him that keeping the public aghast and agog for any length of time is no simple undertaking.

In the Eye of the Beholder

The beauty shop where I go once a week to have my gray locks coiffed, caters almost exclusively to an elderly clientele. There is no doubt a limited amount that can be done for me, but still, I emerge feeling happier and more self-confident because I've done all I can to keep up appearances. I feel more socially acceptable.

The need to try to accommodate to the popular standards of beauty, no matter what one's age, makes me glad that I do not live in a society where attractiveness is measured by the size of the discs implanted in my lips, or the number of brass rings used to elongate my neck, or the artistic complexity of elaborate facial tattoos. Things are hard enough as it is!

One of the patrons of a salon I once visited was a lady who had remained frozen in the past. She sought to maintain an image of herself as she appeared in her hey-day without recognizing that she had altered from the fashionable slimness of her younger years into skinny old age. But, osteoporosis notwithstanding, she tottered into the salon in her retro springolator pumps and a sleeveless, close-fitting sheath dress. After her white hair was colored to an approximation of the bright blond of yester-year, it was teased into the bouffant style she favored. Alas, sometimes we are unaware that we may have transmogrified from a "vision of sheer delight" into an unsettling apparition.

Now why is it, I wonder to myself, that we started decorating and embellishing --- and often disfiguring ourselves--- in the first place? Was it through boredom, or insecurity or an effort to go Mother Nature one better, that we invented a kind of walking graffiti? I am aware that psychologists and anthropologists have developed exhaustively complex theories concerning this question, mostly having to do with mating rituals, tribal dominance, the thirst for eternal youth, and an innate desire either to stand out, or *not* stand out, in a crowd. Whatever the reason, things have gotten out of hand.

If one stops to consider all the products and services available for feminine personal enhancement, the mind reels. On the least sophisticated level there are moderately priced, simple lotions, potions,

31

soaps, unguents, and powders which end up costing plenty because we purchase many, if not all, of them. From there we proceed to complex beauty products which must be rigorously tested on hapless rabbits before being marketed to women who pay a great deal of money for a very few ounces of a celebrity-labeled, exotically packaged, nice smelling product declared safe to use.

Additionally, for varying amounts of capital outlay, there are gyms with personal trainers and space-age equipment to help build magnificent bodies, and spas offering massages and scented steamy baths to produce gorgeous, relaxed bodies. Then if the socially ideal beautiful appearance has still not been achieved, there is plastic surgery which offers tucks, lifts, and implants here and there to meet fashion's specifications. I will not elaborate on such procedures as depilation, dermabrasion, and cellulite suctioning.

Since I am well into my ninth decade, I do not spend time worrying about how to avail myself of all these things, let alone pay for them. I do not aspire to a beauty make-over since I certainly no longer have suitable raw material for such an enterprise. Besides, it's the sort of thing that could kill a person. One of my contemporaries is convinced that when one is old, one fades into a kind of obscurity and becomes socially invisible. If this is true, I don't necessarily need to have my hair done every week. On the other hand I do still look in the mirror, and I want to see someone I can relate to. I suspect the lady in the springolator shoes is seeking the same thing. It's just that she's looking a little farther back than I am.

Calendar Entries

Over the last few years my daily calendar has undergone a gradual change. Interspersed among the dates marked for club meetings, lunch and dinner engagements, visits by out of town guests, weddings, projected excursions and vacation trips, and the birthdays of family and friends, there are notations of a far different sort. They read: Ruth's biopsy, Dave's MRI, Jean's echo cardiogram, Paul's laser surgery, Bob's knee replacement, and Anne's cataract operation. These medical events increasingly vie with social events for space in the neat little squares I mark to keep my life organized.

When, with considerable trepidation, I call my friends and ask in my most up-beat tone of voice, "Well, how did it go?" I pray they will respond:

"No problem. All the test results came back negative." Or,

"Laser surgery is a piece of cake!" Or,

"My doc says I'll be back to square dancing in no time!" Or,

"You may not believe this, but my vision is already better than it's been in years-and without glasses." Or,

"I was scared to death, but my heart is just fine. I can cross that worry off my list!"

These positive replies reassure my friends and me that the glitches in our aging physical machinery can be repaired, that keeping healthy is a matter of careful maintenance. Once again, we can lock the specter of mortality back into a closed compartment in our minds. We marvel at the advances in medical science. We rejoice that we live where wonderful care is available to us. We make a date for lunch to celebrate life, and health and the gift of time together, as well we should.

Then one day when I make a check-up call to a dear friend who has been undergoing some tests, mortality answers the telephone. A "mass" has been discovered, "metastasis" has occurred, treatment will not alter the condition, hospice has been called. And although reason has told me some time ago that this might happen, my breathing nevertheless stops. This is cruel, unjust! How can it be that an unrelenting sentence has been so quickly passed upon my friend! Only last week this vital, creative and generous person had lent me her support when I was troubled by a difficult problem. Uncertain, knowing the inadequacy of anything I can do, I ask, "Would it be all right if I stop by for a little while?" I take her a loaf of zucchini bread and small bouquet of roses.

My meeting is awkward with this cherished companion whose days have abruptly dwindled "down to a precious few." We regard each other with stricken eyes, wordlessly embrace. "Oh, damn!" I finally say in a shaky voice.

"You're so right," she replies

Death is the intrusive third party who sits with us, inhibiting our usual easy interchange, stifling any tendency towards laughter and the plain silliness we have always enjoyed together.

We have entered a time of leave-taking. Diffidently, and acutely aware of my own weaknesses, I accompany her as best I can on some stages of her final journey. She is surrounded and supported by a sensitive and loving family and she reaches out for spiritual guidance from her church. She receives steadfast care and counseling from hospice. I am moved and humbled by her growing strength and calm as she approaches the end of her life. I also grow. Incredibly, we find ourselves laughing together once again. There is heightened kindness and a perfect truthfulness in what we say to each other.

One day she says, "We all have to die, don't we?" and I answer, "Yes, we do." But I'm not sure either of us quite believes it, although I know she is much nearer acceptance than I am. Part of me is clamoring, "No, not yet. Please, not yet."

At what turns out to be our last good-bye, she says, "I have always loved you."

"I love you, too," I respond with my whole heart.

The date of her memorial service is noted in one of my calendar squares. As she requested, "The Ode to Joy" will be sung.

The Good Provider

When my father was old and frail he sat on our patio every morning awaiting the arrival of Freddie the Freeloader. He kept a sack of cracked corn in his lap and as soon as Freddie arrived, he scattered a small handful of it on the table beside him. Freddie, in his cautious way conducted a brief aerial surveillance for any hostile elements (cats) in the vicinity before he flew down from the garage roof for breakfast. He cooed a greeting to my father as he pecked away at his morning repast.

My father's conversation with Freddie usually began, "Well, you're right on time again this morning," to which Freddie would respond with a soft "oo-coo-roo."

"You're a smart old bird, aren't you? Never pass up a hand-out, do you?" A head-bobbing "oo-coo-roo," from a preoccupied Freddie who was methodically consuming every minute fragment provided for him.

"No sense working for a living, is there? Not when you've got some old guy who's willing to give you something for nothing."

"Oo-coor-oo!"

But Freddie, whose name we had borrowed from a Red Skelton comic character, while not exactly working for a living, was nevertheless giving a great deal. When he made his pigeon-toed way across the table and perched on the back of my father's chair and cooed in his ear, he was offering his trust to a weary, white-haired gentleman whose world had become very small. Feeding Freddie gave a purpose to my father's days. It enabled him to continue his long-time role as the good provider. He had taken responsibility for a needy bird, a bedraggled avian specimen who had not kept up with the flock. Perhaps Freddie had been through about as much in his lifetime as my father had been in his. They did seem to understand each other.

Whenever this particular memory of my father comes to mind, it typifies for me his matter of fact kindness and easy generosity. He would have been the last person on earth to preach to my brother and me that "it's more blessed to give than to receive." He was not a man who lived by adages nor did he want special recognition for what he gave. He was a practical man who felt an obligation to extend a helping hand when it was needed.

My brother and I were orphans, age seven and four, when he and our mother-to-be took us from the Wyoming state children's home to be their own. Their unspoken commitment to us was the same commitment they had made aloud to each other on their wedding day, "for better or for worse, for richer or for poorer, in sickness and in health."

Our mother, who had been one of twelve children, regarded selfishness as one of the cardinal sins. Our father sometimes smiled at her when she scolded us for showing signs of greed, or a reluctance to share. He himself was always prepared "to give anybody the shirt off his back," as our mother pointed out to us.

His own childhood was one of unrelenting hard labor as he struggled along with his German immigrant parents to survive on their Nebraska homestead. I have often thought that if anything would make a person stingy, it would be growing up under conditions where every bite of food was so hard won. But his attitude was directly opposite to that; his greatest enjoyment lay in inviting people to our home and feeding them. This included friends, relatives, and the stream of traveling salesmen who called on him at his store. Fortunately he and my mother were in perfect accord in this respect, and she found it no hardship to put another board in the table to accommodate extras.

When my brother arrived home with a new-born puppy, one of a litter his boy scout patrol had found abandoned in a ditch when they were out hiking, my father commented, "It takes a mighty hard heart to throw away helpless little animals." After putting in a ten-hour day at his store, he was the one who got out of bed at night when the puppy whimpered to feed it a special formula from a small nursing bottle. Our puppy was the only survivor from the litter. He grew into a huge, ungainly, yellow animal completely unsuited for life on a city lot. My father eventually found a rancher who was willing to take him and he spent happy years loping across the prairie in pursuit of rabbits.

The lines on my father's face grew deep during the bitter years of the depression. He often drove to work through the dust storms which added to the general misery. Brown billows blurred the sun and robbed the color from Wyoming's skies. Precious topsoil, blown all the way from Oklahoma, powdered our hair and clothes, sifted into houses and stores and gritted on the city streets. Nevertheless, his music and stationery store opened six mornings every week, as clean and orderly as it was humanly possible to keep it; and somehow he managed to maintain his business without laying-off any of his employees.

My mother turned the worn collars on his shirts and patched the tattered linings of his suit coats. My brother and I had little concept of the corners our parents were cutting, or of the heroic daily struggle to provide for us. We were loved, and our father was with us every day, teasing us, hugging us, bragging about our accomplishments and encouraging us to take another stab at the things we found hard to do. What more did we need? Like Freddie the Freeloader, we had it made.

I wish I had understood enough to coo in my father's ear, the way Freddie did.

Turmoil in Eden

The garden section of my Saturday newspaper carried a picture of a lady standing serene among the shoulder-high Jerusalem artichokes in her garden. She is obviously of a calmer disposition than I am. A display of such rampant growth is always a source of consternation to me. I am unnerved when nature is so far out of control.

When visitors enter my garden, they describe it as restful, peaceful, idyllic. They are soothed, they say. However when I stroll the paths, I know I am surrounded by pockets of anarchy, sinister underground activities, fierce resistance movements, and imminent hostile take-overs. Actually my garden has become a battle ground.

Consider my climbing Cecile Brunner rose. This was planted as a dainty little sprig to twine delicately about my pergola. It started out modestly enough, but within a couple of seasons, it abandoned all restraint, and despite vigorous pruning on numerous occasions, it has maintained such an appetite for dominance that it can be held in check only by wielding a chain saw.

Then there are the violets. This flower was invented to inspire poets, and truly I was captivated by the first little violet blooms in my yard and considered writing an ode or two. Then as violets began appearing hither and yon in all my flower beds, in my lawn, between stepping stones and in my crannied walls, I became disenchanted, dismayed, desperate and furious, in that order. I first attacked these wee plants with a pointed trowel, progressed to a multi-pronged cultivator and am now digging ever deeper with a heavy duty spading fork. A trencher is next, I suppose.

Whenever I read a garden magazine article describing any plant that spreads by stolons, I cannot repress a shudder. What comes to mind is a Chinese Lantern (only one plant you understand) that a friend gave me. Within a few short weeks of setting it out, I was amazed to discover that it had traveled a half city block, with a series of little plantlets connected on a long string, just like Christmas tree lights. When I recovered from my fright, I began uprooting these at warp speed clear back to the source, and yes, I admit it, I poisoned the mother plant.

I have become wary of people who offer to share plants. It stands to reason that what they are eager to share is a prolific grower--- like Lady Bells--- otherwise, why would they appear in their pick-up truck with large cardboard boxes overflowing with plants? Within a few months after tucking a few Lady Bells into one of my flower beds, I understood that these are no ladies. They are a wanton bunch. What Chinese Lanterns do above ground, Lady Bells do under-ground. Their off-spring are made immortal by an ineradicable root system as complex as a neural network.

My eye falls on the Peruvian lilies. The original plants were gifts which I received with gladness. They are lovely. Then I note that the gorgeous red one is about to meet up with the gorgeous yellow one in a pincers movement designed to strangle a very expensive Japanese maple. I begin pulling up flower stems like a woman possessed while making soothing clucking noises to the hapless maple which is facing a slow death by suffocation.

Ground covers are highly recommended as a way to conserve moisture, prevent erosion, and forestall weeds. Accordingly I have planted Sweet Woodruff, Cranesbill Geraniums and Lysemachia . Alas, megalomania has set in. These plants have mobilized to cover the earth. A friend of mine who is a relative of Mrs. Malaprop once created the word "engulp" when what she meant was engulf. I can tell you that my ruffled petunias are being engulped even as we speak.

Last week a visitor exclaimed, "I would never go in the house if I were surrounded by an Eden such as this!"

And I replied, "Well, yes, I do spend most of my time outdoors." I did not explain that I'm afraid to turn my back on my garden. A person could be engulped you know.

Wyoming Easter

Springtime in Wyoming was always a very iffy thing. Nevertheless after a few balmy days in a row, my mother and the crocuses usually came out together, beguiled once again into believing that winter was over. Despite years of discouraging meteorological data, my mother began laying plans for a "nice Easter." She never fully accepted that Mother Nature, while enchanting, also has a mean streak in her, and might decide to whip up gale force winds or a full scale blizzard for Easter Sunday.

But no matter what the weather might be, Easter outfits were still of primary importance. My mother always had visions of how she wanted me to look. Generally speaking this was all right with me. I liked new clothes and shiny patent leather shoes and I had every expectation of fitting right in with all the other 8-year old girls in my Sunday school class. We might arrive at church in winter coats and galoshes, but we would have bows in our hair. Underneath the heavy coats we would be wearing the lace-trimmed dotted Swiss or flowered dimity dresses our mothers had made for us.

However, a friend of the family unexpectedly sent me a dress. It came all the way from the Philippine Islands where she and her army officer husband were stationed. The dress was pure white, lavishly embroidered in bright blue around the neck and sleeves and hemline, and it had a tasseled draw-string at the waist. Mother, an expert needlewoman herself, was in raptures over the exquisite, complex embroidery, and declared that I was the most fortunate of little girls to have such a lovely dress. I was aghast. I had never seen anything remotely like it before---it looked foreign, and I felt peculiar in it. Young herd animal that I was, I wanted to look exactly like my friends.

I knew there was absolutely no way to explain to mother that I hated the dress, and any show of petulance was impermissible. I had learned that in certain circumstances bowing to authority was my only feasible option.

Mother decided that the dress required a hat to complete its effect. This entailed a visit to Miss Cottingham's Millinery Shoppe

41

which was a hushed and carpeted place, somewhat like the funeral parlor I had once been in, a place for final arrangements.

The hats were displayed on small stands atop tables. Mother flitted about like a hummingbird among flowers, while Miss Cottingham followed behind her with the rapt patience of a stalking cat. A white hat of "superior quality Milan straw" was placed upon my head. After negotiating a change of ribbon streamers to exactly match the blue in my dress, a transaction was completed.

Easter morning dawned fair, sparkling and almost warm. Mother was ecstatic as our family set off on the walk to church. My older brother and I walked in front, followed by our parents. We looked like the ideal happy family, although this was only three-quarters true. I was miserable.

My darkest misgivings proved warranted. When I entered the Sunday school room, all chattering ceased and my contemporaries eyed me in shocked silence. However my Sunday school teacher greeted me with utmost warmth. "Hello, dear, how nice you look. I'll bet your pretty dress came from the Philippines." She turned to the class and continued, "Remember how we've talked about the missionaries our church sends to the Philippine Islands, where people are often so poor they don't have enough to eat? And yet, just imagine, they can find happiness in making beautiful things." Our class really respected missionaries and some of us thought we might someday become missionaries ourselves. Suddenly I was seen in a whole new, quasi-glamorous light. I was after all clothed in an exotic garment made by people in a far-away place, brave people who needed our help.

As our family, now 100% happy, emerged from the church, my hat was snatched from my head by a sudden powerful gust of wind, seemingly coming from nowhere. Streamers flying behind it, the hat whirled upward, then gyrated erratically downward, to impale itself on the bare branch of a lilac bush. When my brother retrieved it, the hat was found to have sustained only a minor puncture wound----due no doubt to its being a "Milan straw of superior quality."

Mother Nature had, however, reminded us that she was still in charge and could have made things a whole lot worse if she had really wanted to.

42

Common Courtesy

Wyoming has long been known as the land of "wide open spaces." When I was growing up in Cheyenne in the 1930's, crowd control was the least of anybody's worries. We took our elbow room for granted and we knew we could always find a seat at any public gathering, with the possible exception of the local theater when the bank night jack-pot reached a staggering high of $400 and you had to be present to win.

Although we knew about the congestion in large cities, we, personally, couldn't relate to it. If friends mentioned they might take a trip to New York, they were jokingly advised: "Don't ever fall down in New York City. The people there won't help you up, they'll just step over you---if you're lucky." There was awareness, even then, when the U.S. population was a mere 125 million, that there is an inverse relationship between population density and human civility. (Although the national population is now close to 307 million, Wyoming remains the least populous state in the Union and still has plenty of space. Do you suppose it therefore follows that Wyoming's residents are the most polite people in the USA?)

Anyway, you can understand how astonished I was as a young bride, in 1942, to find myself suddenly transplanted from Cheyenne to Los Angeles to begin married life. My new husband had grown up on a dry farm in Colorado, and as he herded cows and shucked corn, he dreamed of building airplanes. When he was seventeen he headed for California and The Lockheed Aircraft Corporation. After a year of training in aircraft school, he was hired as an experimental mechanic.

By the time we were married, he had lived in Hollywood and then in Burbank for four years, and had become a man- about- town, so to speak. He was absolutely overjoyed at the prospect of introducing me to all the marvels he had discovered in Los Angeles. The only problem was that it was war-time and he was working 12-hour shifts, six days a week. There was also the matter of gasoline rationing.

However, every Sunday morning, we boarded street-cars and buses and made multiple transfers to go to the beach at Santa Monica

43

or to visit the Griffith Park zoo, the county museum, the La Brea tar pits, Grauman's Chinese theater, or China town and Olvera Street, in downtown Los Angeles, where I ate the first "foreign" food I ever tasted. He also, in a misguided moment, introduced me to department stores, which to my dazzled eyes rivaled the fabled treasure troves of the Indies. We loved Los Angeles then, when it had around three million residents, and continued to enjoy it for almost forty years more, as the population gradually swelled to almost nine million!

It was not until we both retired from our careers, that we acknowledged that Los Angeles was not as user friendly as it once was. The freeways had become the "fear-ways" and everything we did was increasingly time-consuming and complex. Like so many other retirees, we headed for the hills, or in our case, the Sierra foothills. We moved to Grass Valley, California, where, in the fifteen years before his death, my husband and I found delight in the beauty around us, and the excitement of changing seasons. We also formed some of the strongest friendships of our lives. After I became a widow, I stayed on in a community where I knew somebody would help me up if I happened to fall down.

And sure enough, last week in a local department store, I was reaching up to a high shelf to check out the size of a pair of jeans I thought might be right for my son. The whole towering stack of Levis slipped off the shelf and tumbled down on top of me, catching me off-balance. A young woman shopping nearby rushed over, exclaiming "Oh, I hope you're not hurt! My goodness, let me help you up!" She pushed the Levis aside with the speed and vigor of someone rescuing a victim from the rubble after an earthquake. She looked me over carefully to assess any possible damage (none), straightened the collar on my shirt and picked two gray hairs off the shoulder of my black sweater. "Now what size are you looking for? Maybe I can help you find it." And she did. Now is that civility, or what!

Showing Our Colors

We have become accustomed to ladies appearing all over the country in red hats, sometimes worn with purple dresses. These are women of mature years; most of them are white-haired. When they arrive in a group at a restaurant or an art gallery or a theater, they seem to descend like a flock of tropical birds. They are chattering and laughing, obviously enjoying themselves. They are, of course, members of the Red Hat Society, the loosely structured organization which has rapidly gained nation-wide popularity. Their stated purpose is to have a good time. They make the reckless assertion that it's o.k. to take a little time off from their volunteer activities at the hospital or the library or the food bank and just have some fun—and to look gaudy while they are doing it, no matter what their age.

This is a pretty heady concept for a person like me who was brought up to believe that it's improper to call attention to oneself, and who was further admonished to always "act your age." At eighty-six, I do not look like a babushka exactly, but on the other hand I do wear conservative, tailored clothes in neutral, interchangeable colors which I sometimes daringly enliven with a scarf or a bit of jewelry. In other words, I fade into whatever background I happen to be in. You will not be surprised to learn that I have not joined a Red Hat Society.

However, these women have caused me to give some thought to color and how we use it to make a statement about our lives. The Red Hat ladies seem to be saying, "Look at us! We're all dressed up! These are difficult and scary times, but over the years we've been through plenty, and we're still around to tell you joy has not vanished from the earth."

An artist friend of mine who made a serious study of folk art concluded that the poorer a country is, the brighter the colors its artisans use. I don't know if she confirmed some universal truth, but I do understand how color can lift our hearts.

Last week in the mail I received a sale catalog of women's clothing. As I leafed through it, my attention was caught by a very full skirt, tiered in wide bands of brilliant pink, red, and orange. It looked like something one would wear to a fiesta or put on to dance the can-

can. Carmen Miranda would have liked it. I did, too. It made me think what fun it would be to kick up my heels, or at least flounce about for a bit clicking castanets. I studied the skirt with the kind of dreamy desire I have not felt since I shopped with my mother for my junior prom dress. I tried to imagine what occasion on my social calendar could justify my ordering anything so outlandish: None. Even in my manic, delusional state, I realized the skirt would not look the same on me as it did on the lithe young model in the catalog. I also conceded that the effect would undoubtedly border on the bizarre.

Nevertheless, I wanted it.

An inner dialog with my conservative, rational self ensued: "Have you totally lost your wits?"

"No, not at all. What's wrong with wearing something bright and gay, for a change?"

"For Pete's sake, act your age! There's no more pathetic sight than an old woman trying to act young and giddy!"

"Well, I *feel* young!"

"That's not the same as *looking* young or *being* young. For heaven's sake, get real. I am not prepared to deal with some kind of nut case." (My rational self is pretty plain-spoken.)

With a sigh, I put the catalog aside, but I have kept it on my bedside table after turning down the corner of the page with the skirt on it. Sometimes I peek at that page and I have this almost irresistible urge to pick up the telephone and order the skirt. But I've had the catalog for over a week, and it says on the cover that "quantities are limited." They've probably sold all of the skirts by now.

If I were a Red Hat lady I would take a chance and make the call anyway.

Where Am I?

Like the poet, A.E. Housman, I sometimes feel I'm "a stranger and afraid / in a world I never made." This lost feeling most often sweeps over me when I 'm dealing with an ATM machine, a self-service gas pump or an automated phone system. These things seem to do what they're supposed to do for countless other people but not for me. Even if I study all the written instructions beforehand, or listen carefully and even replay the recorded instructions (or menu) two or three times, the minute I push a button on anything, or insert a card, the whole system falls apart. Part of the difficulty stems from my not hearing or seeing as well as I did a few years ago. And, yes, perhaps I am now synaptically challenged when it comes to grasping new concepts. But I am earnest and certainly well-meaning and I always put forth my best effort before technical assistance is called for by me, or some frustrated by-stander.

At the ATM machine, I have had a queue of muttering people, not unlike a lynch mob, form behind me, openly wondering why on earth it's taking me so long to accomplish a simple transaction. I often receive an accusatory look from the technician who has been summoned to straighten out whatever glitch I have introduced into a heretofore reliable program. It is as if I have wantonly injured a member of his immediate family.

Have you ever noticed how brusque and impatient people may become when they are explaining a simple, to them, technology to someone who doesn't understand it at all and never in her wildest imaginings expected to have to contend with it? The niceties of human behavior tend to be disregarded when we are dealing with technical matters. Perhaps this is because kindness is apt to be time consuming and the whole point of our automated and mechanized world is to speed up transactions and thereby save us time to engage in more time-saving activities.

Last week I felt a familiar lurch in the pit of my stomach when I encountered an automated check-out system in a huge home and garden store. There was an assistant positioned near-by to help the inexperienced, but she looked downright hostile. And why wouldn't she be? She was assisting the store to phase out her job, along with

47

those of all the live people tending the soon to be outdated row of check-out stations where the doomed employees were greeting customers with a friendly, "Good morning, how are you?" Machines, I reflected, do not require coffee breaks and have no need to laugh and talk with each other and inquire, "How's it going for you today?" Naturally I by-passed the automated check-out and stood in line for the services of a human checker. I wondered if the checker knew she was a member of an endangered species, that her days were numbered.

Recently I took a trip with my daughter which involved some time spent on rapid transit. Once again I experienced a sense of acute estrangement. I suddenly realized that I would never travel any place again without someone along to press the right buttons on one of the battery of change machines, and then proceed to another set of computerized machines to procure the correct ticket for our desired destination. If this whole procedure had been left to me, I would still be standing on the wrong side of the turnstile while streams of the technologically savvy went clicking past.

Without intending to sound boastful, I can honestly say that most of the time I have had reason to consider myself a fairly sharp-witted old lady. And yet when I'm caught in the toils of an unforgiving system that must be programmed without the slightest deviation in order to function at all, and which is meant to hurry me along like a tin can on a conveyor belt, I become disoriented and lose track of where I am and what it was I set out to do.

Do you think it's possible that many of the elderly who have been diagnosed as victims of Alzheimer's disease are instead suffering from technology trauma, a poorly understood condition closely related to battle fatigue?

Applying for a Grant from
The Gates Foundation

Recent television interviews of Bill Gates as he announced his retirement from Microsoft have once again shown him to be a sincere, modest, happy-natured family man. Through the Gates Foundation he has declared his intention to share his vast wealth to make the world a better place. Who can quarrel with his philanthropic intent or deny his commitment? One can only admire Bill's prodigious talent and strive to emulate his creative, hard-working ways. Aside from the late beloved Mr. Rogers, there is no one else one can think of who would be more welcome in anybody's neighborhood.

On the other hand, it is well to remember that Bill Gates also conceived of his gigantic Microsoft Corporation as a vehicle for improving our overall quality of life. In many ways he has no doubt succeeded, probably beyond even his wildest dreams, but in the process he has also drastically altered our lifestyle and thereby created some areas of utter desolation.

The thing is, Bill is a genius, which means that he is congenitally incapable of recognizing that other people, even those who have heretofore been judged mentally competent, often find it impossible to follow his thought processes. A genius never seems to realize how much smarter he is than other people, especially when he is surrounded by cadres of other geniuses (and young nerdish children!) who *do* appear to understand most of what he's talking about. Bear in mind that Gates enjoys high-level, recreational chess and that he becomes rhapsodic when talking about soft-ware applications which are far more mystifying and multi-dimensional than chess is. Accept that he will undoubtedly be remembered as the Franz Liszt of the computer world; he began with what now appears to be a simple theme and developed variations of dizzying complexity which he then generously invited others to go ahead and play.

The truth is that Bill Gates, in all innocence and without any apparent misgivings, has been guilty of destroying the serenity and self-confidence of a large segment of our population. He has locked a whole host of us innocuous elderly people into a window-filled cyber-

49

structure where the views we encounter are not only unfamiliar but strangely menacing. We become disoriented. With mounting panic we search for guidance. We turn to the emergency automated telephones provided for our convenience, only to have our feeble cries for help answered by remote, flat-voiced technicians who interpret the scenes before us in language we have never heard before. They advise us to study the signs posted all around us which they feel we ought to be able to read, because we know, or can at least sound out phonetically, what the words are. But the words form a context somehow indecipherable to us. Terrified, we search for the exit to the structure, only to come at last to the Kafka-esque realization that there *is* no way out. We are doomed to technology.

Nevertheless, human nature being what it is, one still seeks salvation. Perhaps the remedy for our isolation and enslavement lies within the Gates Foundation itself. Maybe what is needed is to solicit the sponsorship of the AARP and then employ a talented grant- writer, one who is of course fully competent in the Microsoft Word program, to document our plight and request assistance from the Foundation's board of directors. Surely any institution dedicated to humanitarian aims must respond to the plea that the survival of the elderly depends upon at least a partial return to the slower-paced simplicity of yesteryear.

Our modest proposal might include the reinstatement of a universally reliable type of telephone with a live operator who could put us in direct touch with a kindly advisor who would speak to us in unaccented English, using a revised technological nomenclature which includes such understandable words as "doohickey" and "thingamajig". Is this too much to ask?

My Love Lies Dreaming

Seventy two years ago, when I was age fourteen, I fell deeply in love with a whole lot of men, all at the same time. The roster included Clark Gable, Gary Cooper, Charles Boyer, the boys' junior high school P-E teacher, the University of Wyoming basketball coach, the clerk at the corner grocery store and the baritone soloist in the Congregational church choir.

I had actual pictures of Clark Gable, Gary Cooper, Charles Boyer and the University of Wyoming basketball coach. These were newspaper clippings which were concealed under the flowered paper that lined the top drawer of my dresser. I peeked at them every night. I never personally met any of these hidden loves, of course. But, on the other hand, I saw the grocery store clerk almost daily, and caught sight of the P-E teacher when I was in gym class. On Sunday mornings in church I was free to sit in rapture, which had nothing to do with religious ecstasy, and study the baritone soloist. In any chance encounter with one of the locals, I smiled at them in passing and they smiled back, never suspecting the amorous turmoil they left in their wake. Nor did my family or friends have any inkling of my covert, one-sided love life.

When I was growing up it did not do to be thought of as "boy crazy." One girl I knew, the first one in our class to wear lip stick, the one who later had a glamour job as usherette at the local movie theater, was forthright in her interest in boys. My brother sarcastically dismissed her as someone who "would fall for any guy around, even if he was a yellow dog with red pants on." My mother placed great stress on my being "ladylike" and this certainly did not include any blatant self-promotion or coquettish behavior. My father praised me for being "level-headed," and my teachers considered me a conscientious student. So, like Walter Mitty, I turned to fantasy. In my private world, I was not exactly Lady Chatterley, but, despite my inexperience, I did my best.

A daring innovation in the Cheyenne junior high school curriculum was a class in social usage which was designed to prepare us ninth grade girls for the perils of high school. The class was taught by Miss Elwood, a white-haired maiden lady with prominent teeth who had somehow been up-rooted from the Deep South and inexplicably ended up in Wyoming. She spoke to us about afternoon teas, cotillions, the proper order for introducing one person to another and the gracious way to accept or decline an invitation. She advised us to always remember to put hand lotion on our elbows because if we omitted this step from our toilette, we could end up with calloused elbows which would negate any possible charm we might otherwise have had. In addition, she exhorted us to "keep smiling." This would help us through practically all embarrassments. It was especially important to smile if you needed to excuse yourself from a social gathering to go to the bathroom.

The word "sex" never passed Miss Elwood's lips. Her sole advice on dating was for us to encourage only gentlemanly young fellows who understood how to treat a real lady. A review of all the boys I knew did not reveal anybody answering this description. I took refuge in my own stable of glamour men.

The constrictions of my adolescence, when viewed by today's lenient standards, seem absurd. I simply grew up in a time when we were never allowed any slack because of our "raging hormones." Sexual freedom absolutely did not apply to our age group and if anyone had suggested sex education beginning in our sixth grade class, there would have been multiple cases of cardiac arrest among our parents. Nor did our families accept the teen age years as a period set aside for unconventional or rebellious behavior. We were viewed as awkward kids, not yet "dry behind the ears," who needed firm guidance to reach responsible maturity by the time we "came of age" at twenty-one. This was not a perfect system and did not always produce the results intended. I do not expect to live long enough to see if today's relaxed ways will result in a better outcome.

I can only tell you that my elbows still look okay and I found lasting happiness with a gentlemanly fellow who looked a lot like the Wyoming University basket ball coach.

Out of Tune and Out-Numbered

When people tell us we can accomplish anything we want to if we try hard enough, they mean well, but they are sometimes quite wrong. I have spent a lifetime struggling unsuccessfully to overcome two serious learning deficits.

First of all, I am a lost cause, musically speaking. Melodies do not strike my ear and linger pleasantly in my mind the way they do with other people. I cannot carry a tune and, for me, rhythm is merely an intellectual concept.

Secondly, I find anything having to do with numbers downright arcane. For example, there is a perpetual irreconcilable difference between my bank statement and my check register, no matter how painstakingly I calculate.

Researchers have located specific sites in the brain responsible for musical and mathematical aptitude. For this reason, I have resolved never to have a brain scan of any sort. I have no wish to be revealed as a medical oddity with a cerebrum as riddled with holes as a Swiss cheese, or, worse yet, perhaps one with a whole hemisphere atrophied to the size of a prune.

My musical education, which I entered into with the utmost good will, began at age six. My adoptive mother, who had always yearned to play the piano, saw to it that I received the music lessons she was denied. Neither my eager young music teacher nor I had the least premonition of the struggle that lay ahead. I easily learned to read single notes, fascinated by the small bug-like forms that crawled about among the lines of the bass and treble clefs, but when the time came to combine these notes, I was incapable of discerning when I had hit a wrong note except by the restrained gurgles of my teacher or by my mother's more overt cries. Furthermore, I had no sense of rhythm. When my teacher asked, "Honey, don't you feel the beat?" I didn't know what she was talking about. Like Sigmund Freud, who did not care for music, I felt nothing and heard only "musical noise."

You might suppose that my mother could have accepted that I simply had some gaps in my circuitry, but, alas, no. Dreams die hard. She was a determined and optimistic woman who believed that with

53

training and practice some dormant musical ability would awaken in me. I certainly did not want to disappoint my brand-new, lovely mother. I can honestly tell you I put my all into learning to play the piano.

After a while I learned to sight read pretty well, but since I never had any real idea of what should come next, each time I played a piece it was a new adventure. Tempo remained an iffy concept, inversely related to the complexity of whatever composition I was attempting. When attending to runs, trills, arpeggios and grace notes, timing fell by the wayside.

Memorizing music was out of the question save for one notable exception. After seven or eight years of lessons, I could play, "Believe Me If All Those Endearing Charms" from memory. And I still can. I have no idea why.

As to mathematics, my troubles began in the first grade. Once again, I started out with a genuinely positive attitude. I liked the looks of numbers, particularly fours, which I had once seen written with the top of the four closed into a triangular shape so that it looked like a little sail boat. I persisted in writing my fours that way until the teacher complained to my mother and I was told to produce a standardized version. This convinced me that there is no room for whimsicality when you're dealing with arithmetic. It was an uphill journey from there.

Nevertheless I survived the years of basic arithmetic with the kind of stoicism we reserve for coping with chronic illness, and actually clawed my way through first year geometry. Reprieve finally came when my high school math teacher implored me not to sign up for algebra. After our geometry experience, she figured both of us had suffered enough.

I once heard mathematics described as a study of "pure cold beauty." It sounded to me as if they were talking about graveyard statuary. Frankly, I am more attracted to things that are warm and fuzzy. As a matter of fact, "Believe Me If All Those Endearing Young Charms" has a kind of warm and fuzzy quality about it, don't you think?

Primrose Path

An array of primroses strikes the eye like a box of newly opened crayons. The colors are basic and pure. The blossoms are also basic, a design so simple it might have been invented by a child. **Primroses 4-inch pots $1.29** the super-market sign proclaims. The spectacle of a hundred flats of primroses in bloom next to the market's asphalt parking lot becomes an unexpected site for an ode to joy. I feel like William Wordsworth did when he caught sight of the "host of daffodils."

I have a few primroses in my yard at home, but I am smitten by this year's new, fresh crop. I choose two pots, one with a plant with a bright yellow flower with a heart of dark gold; the other pot holds two plants, one has a deep maroon flower with a yellow center, the other plant a blossom of plain bright blue.

The primroses in my yard have bloomed bravely and sporadically all winter long. I planned to divide my plants, thereby expanding my primrose population at no extra cost and establishing my own primrose path which I could lead somebody down, or better yet, somebody could lead *me* down. But alas, the deer who reside in the lower half of my yard decided that this year, primroses are on their menu----they didn't touch them last year. They daintily nibbled their destructive way through many of the plants in my unfenced front yard.

However primroses are tough, small and pretty, but tough in a very nice way, like some single mothers I have known. They are now sending up new shoots and some are full of buds preparing to flower again. The plants are smaller and more compact than before, as if they are restraining any tendency to extravagant over-growth, having discovered that the world is a hazardous place and that it's better to keep a low profile.

If I were a philosopher I could undoubtedly develop a whole new perspective by contemplating these doughty, wee plants. But as it is, I merely smile upon my two new plants and decide to pick up ten more. What the heck! At these prices I can afford to intersperse new plants among the old ones. We have to take some chances in life, and besides, when it comes to surviving adversity, primroses are proven performers. I plant them with pleasure and contemplate them with delight.

Then my semi-monthly English Garden magazine arrives in the mail. The latest edition arouses my usual feelings of fawning admiration and corrosive envy. I leaf through the pages of visually stunning photographs of the perfectly groomed gardens of the British Isles. They are a-riot with color and are planted so lushly that no patch of bare earth shows any place. I am all too aware that by comparison my garden is meager, even stingy-looking, and marks me as a Scrooge among gardeners. What is needed is a more lavish hand. "Dream large," I say to myself as I head off to the nursery where I purchase two whole flats of primroses!

After a primrose planting blitzkrieg by me and the man who comes once a week to help in my yard, I stand on the deck surveying our efforts. The effect is a pattern of randomly-spaced, vivid dots strewn, like a broken string of beads on a brown carpet. I have not begun to cover the ground and I have discovered a sobering truth. There is no such thing as enough primroses.

It occurs to me that the British have spent centuries developing their gardens. During that time, there have been whole regiments of gardeners devoted to dividing and propagating primroses. This year, knees permitting, I too shall divide my primrose plants. Divide and conquer is probably an old English adage.

To Life

Even when, swatter in hand, I am in pursuit of an especially bothersome fly, I cannot help but recognize how valuable life is to any of its possessors. As soon as the fly is aware that I am bent on its destruction, its flight accelerates to a speed difficult for the human eye to follow and it begins a series of hyperbolic evasive maneuvers to save itself. But since I am the relentless lord high executioner, the most the fly can hope for is a few more seconds of its buzzing existence. Though I may miss in some of my murderous attempts, there is the moment when the swatter hits its target. "Aha! Gotcha!"

Then, unbidden, the perplexing question of predestination comes to my mind. How come I missed on all my other attempts? Was the fly precisely timed to relinquish its vital spark at that one exact moment and no other? Soldiers on the battlefield fatalistically speak of the bullet that has their name or number on it. In our computerized, science fiction age, this kind of minute, cosmic programming seems less and less far-fetched. Most religions are interlaced with the hint that everything about us is fully known, and is kept on file by robed security agents at some undisclosed location.

I can think of no living organism, no matter how microscopic or seemingly defenseless, which does not have an inborn plan for self-preservation. All of us seem to cry out in loud or tiny voices, "I'm here and I am important to the scheme of things; I must live!" This kind of thinking is labyrinthine and unsettling. It leads one into a consideration of the practical difficulties of whole-heartedly subscribing to Albert Schweitzer's philosophy of reverence for life or to the Hindu belief that God is the core of every living thing. (One ends up surrounded by herds of pushy bullocks, rampaging monkeys and biting insects.) It also explains the unease primitive people feel when they kill an animal for food and makes one understand why they ritually thank the dead animal and apologize for taking its life. Some inner voice seems to inform us that depriving anything of its life is no small matter. I long ago acknowledged that if I, personally, had to kill something in order to eat, I would be a vegetarian.

We humans give full attention to staying alive. We strive to increase our longevity by any means available—amulets, pills, nostrums, diet, exercise, meditation, faith healing, medical intervention, and even replacement of diseased organs or worn-out parts. While we may acknowledge the incontrovertible fact of death, we are simultaneously weaving fantasies and theories and belief systems to explain death away. *Other* people may die, and on television we are free to watch them do so every day --- mass murder and genocide are news staples .But *we* are alive. As a completely honest person once said, "I can't imagine the world without *me* in it." Death is not only a mystery, but, I am convinced, it also is a surprise to most of us, no matter how "prepared" we declare ourselves to be.

Since our own lives are so precious to us, how is it that from the beginning of recorded history, from pictograph to television, the theme of the images presented is of slaughter of one kind or another? Bear in mind that according to the story in the book of Genesis, when, one would have to suppose, there were an absolutely minimum number of people on earth, one of them, Cain, killed his brother, Abel. When he was called upon to account for Abel's whereabouts, his petulant non-answer was, "Am I my brother's keeper?" Despite his denial of responsibility, what Cain did was entered in the log book as a crime, or, more biblically, as a sin. And the sin has expanded exponentially over time.

Was there really a particular moment in time when divine programming was in some subtle way altered so that we became the agents for the destruction of our fellow-creatures? As is so often the case, I have no answer to yet another of the knotty questions that has arisen in my mind. And as a born worrier, this could become one more guilt trip for me, although I will probably go on swatting flies.

And speaking of worries, the inner voice I mentioned earlier keeps bringing up Cain's question. I suspect I *do* know the answer to that, and it makes me wish Cain had been an only child.

Lost and Found Department

Recently while doing some research on neurological disorders, I discovered that there is a condition someone has labeled "geographical dyslexia," also known as "directional disability." I have suffered from this syndrome my entire life without realizing that it has a scientific name and has generated scientific study.

Those of us with this affliction can appear normal and self-assured, but are in fact lost most of the time, uncertain which way is left or right, north or south, east or west, although, thank heavens, we can, as a rule, recognize up from down. We are hopeless at either giving or following directions. If we are distracted in any way, getting from point A to point B, even when the trip is one we've made countless times, can result in our arriving at a foreign destination. Any new-comer in town unlucky enough to ask us the way to the post office, may shortly find himself wandering past the city limits.

One of my brothers discovered the extent of my problem when, as an enthusiastic Boy Scout, he attempted to teach me how to tie a square knot. I can still hear him exclaiming, "My gosh! it's just right over left and left over right." Hah!

Sometimes on the school playground and later on in gym class, we marched to commands for right or left turns, or "about face." I considered it a good day if I sometimes chanced to follow directions.

My misguided attempt to learn to square dance resulted in chaos and a tangle of human limbs which disabled an entire square dance group. It is amazing how much confusion is generated when "Allemande right!" and "Allemande left!" are incomprehensible to just one person.

There was also the embarrassing time when I entered my first-born child in kindergarten and the teacher said, "Your little girl is left-handed, isn't she?" and I blurted out, "Oh my goodness, I hadn't noticed."

Naturally, I have developed coping strategies so as to function as competently as possible. When guests telephone to ask for directions for reaching my home (where I have lived for thirty years), I refer to a printed card on my desk with a step by step progression spelled out in bold print. I know any extemporaneous attempt of mine will result in the guests arriving half an hour late because they have had to stop at a fire station or real estate office to ask for help. I also place this kind of printed instruction sheet in plain sight in my car if I am going any place significantly different from my usual daily rounds. If I have a passenger with me, verbal instructions are helpful only if they are offered very slowly, and with no hint of hysteria, to allow me sufficient time to look at my wedding ring and figure out a right versus a left turn.

Maps are of little help to me. After unfolding the map, it takes me a while to decide which way is right side up. Once this has been determined, locating a particular place at a coordinate such as P-15 means nothing to me. My brain cannot apply this diagrammed information to geographic reality. Similarly the large schematic boards erected in shopping malls to aid customers in finding their way about, are confusing to me. Despite the big **X** that proclaims, **You Are Here**, I have been known to ask, "Now just exactly where are we?"

My profound respect for John Steinbeck deepened into outright love when he mentioned in his book, *Travels With Charley,* that he had always had a problem with losing his way and had concluded that he "was born lost and had never been found." I know the feeling!

Fortunately my late husband had the instincts of a homing pigeon and could orient himself to an entire continent with a quick glance at a map. When he became aware of my directional disability, he remarked, "You know, we could take the same vacation every year and it would always be a new experience for you!"

However, now that I realize the scientific community is studying geographical dyslexia, I have taken heart. Since these brilliant minds have figured out how to implant a neat little pacemaker in our chests to keep our hearts ticking along nicely, it seems perfectly reasonable that a Global Positioning System could be inserted in some out of the way groove in our brain. I wonder who I should talk to about this.

Taking Charge

When I was growing up in the 1920's and 1930's, I lived in a household where we were careful in our language. My mother, who was after all, just one-half a generation removed from the Victorian era, placed emphasis on good manners and expected her children to speak with civility at all times. I noticed my mother wince when the family veterinarian once referred to our female Boston terrier as a "nice little bitch."

At age seven I therefore understood that "bitch" had a pejorative connotation and might even be profane. I immediately placed it in my "bad word" file. This designation was further reinforced when my brother was chastised for getting into a fight with his perennial neighborhood enemy and was heard to call him an "SOB!" He actually had to make a full (if insincere) apology to the other boy for having insulted his mother!

You will not be surprised to learn that to this day, eighty years later, "bitch" is not a word that passes my lips with any frequency.

So now we come to Nessie, the splendid Westie I have lived with for eight years. In veterinary parlance I am certain she classifies as a very nice little bitch indeed. As I wrote in a *Bark* article a few years ago, she came to me through the auspices of two dedicated West Highland terrier breeders, Janet and Chuck, who were members of a Scottish dog rescue organization. Before I could qualify as a suitable companion for Nessie, who was recovering from surgery to correct a congenital hip problem, I was intensively interviewed by them, not once but twice, my property was inspected and then modified to meet certain safety standards, and I was required to fill out several pages of paper work. I also signed an agreement to return Nessie to them if I should become unable to care for her. I was then provided with elaborate instructions for this small dog's care and feeding, far more detailed than the ones given to me before I brought my first-born child home from the hospital.

Nessie, I soon understood, is an executive type dog. She recognized an immediate need for a program to organize our daily activities. The regimen she established begins with her arising promptly at seven a.m. and doing a series of stretching and deep breathing exercises performed at my bed-side in order to wake me up. After a flurry of complimentary tail wags and a kiss or two on my limply out-stretched hand, she then briskly requests a few minutes outdoors to check on weather conditions and to chase the squirrels back up into the trees where they belong. She expects that I will be preparing her breakfast during this interval. Following that she nudges me (more about this nudging tendency in just a minute) towards the front door to bring in the morning paper and also to allow her an opportunity to step out on the porch for a full survey of the front yard and surrounding neighborhood. When I pour my morning coffee and she has determined that I am fully awake and functioning as well as I ever do, she considers her duty temporarily done and hops back into her bed to rest for an hour or two. At 9:15 she takes up her position as household guardian at a front window and alerts me to the arrival of the gas company meter reader, the postman, the trash collector, the UPS delivery man, passing pedestrians and also possible guests.

Nessie delights in visitors and always ushers them into the house with joyous barks. She does however require that they come in and sit down and not loiter in the front entry just chatting. She tends to become strident if we do not immediately go into the living room where guests can be properly seated and civilized conversation can begin. She sometimes nudges at my heels to direct me to lead the way – *for pity's sake!*

Now I should tell you that I exchange Christmas cards with Janet, one of my original investigators, and have occasional follow-up calls from her to inquire about Nessie's and my health and the state of our relationship. Janet is a lovely woman who is truly devoted to animal welfare. She is gratified to hear that I am so delighted with Nessie. However, when I recently and in complete innocence, mentioned Nessie's tendency to manage our household schedule, and to nudge at my heels when she wants something done, Janet was horrified. "You must *never* let her do that! That is a *very bad* habit. You must *always* be the one in charge. You absolutely *have* to be the top bitch!"

You can imagine my consternation at this turn of events. The whole thing seems unnatural to me. I am trying to imagine how in the world to break this news to Nessie. And what on earth would my mother think!

Let The Lights Be Burning

Like other prudent householders, I had my flashlight, a box of matches and some candles at hand when the blackout occurred during our recent heavy storm. Since the news media had been warning us for days of the approach of a severe weather system and had reinforced their message with elaborate diagrams and swooping Doppler rays, there could be no possible excuse for lack of preparation.

When the storm struck it seemed to be doing its best to live up to its advance publicity. Rain sheeted over my house. By late afternoon the immense ponderosa pines at the back corner of my yard were no longer pointing skyward but were swaying in great wind-driven arcs and had become possible weapons of mass destruction.

As a safety measure, candles and flashlight in hand, I moved from my dark kitchen to the front room of my house. If one of the trees should fall, I wanted to be as far as possible from its probable trajectory. I was not terrified, but I knew myself to be a vulnerable, and, ah yes, a powerless person alone in my home.

Therefore, you will readily understand how heartened I was to see a flickering light in a window across the street. When I noticed this reassuring sign of life from my nearest neighbor, the chorus from an old hymn I had not thought of for at least seventy years popped into my mind. "Let the lower lights be burning/ Send a gleam along the wave/ Some poor struggling fainting seaman/ You may rescue, you may save!"

What an extraordinary contraption the human brain is! Mine had stored those words away in some remote, unvisited brain cell for decades, and then released them into my consciousness for this precise occasion. Not only did I remember the chorus of the old hymn, but I was also treated to a flood of additional memories including a mental picture of the interior of the old Congregational church in Cheyenne, Wyoming. There I stood along with my parents and the rest of the congregation lustily giving that hymn our all, never mind that we lived high and dry on the prairie, with no seaman, distressed or otherwise, within hundreds of miles of us in any direction. Following this train of thought, I also recalled one of our church soloists, a bass, whose repertoire seemed to be limited to "Rocked in the Cradle of the Deep." The church vibrated around all of us whenever we descended along with him to the ocean floor, but fortunately we were also able to surface with him again to enjoy "calm and peaceful sleep." I have no way of accounting for the popularity of these maritime themes in such incongruous surroundings.

Nevertheless, I do remember emerging from church with a sense of salvation, as if I personally had been snatched from the perils of the sea, and that, as a consequence, it was now up to me to rescue as many struggling, fainting other people as possible. Perhaps this was a beginning of my eventual recognition of how interdependent we human beings are. We simply are not designed to "go it alone."

During the days and nights when the power was out, I kept in touch with friends and family by means of their cell phones and my one telephone that was still working. We compared survival strategies and I envied those who were keeping warm with generators they had installed in their homes. I also relived my early failures as a girl scout; I was never able to build a decent fire. So, of course, when I attempted to kindle a fire in my seldom-used wood stove the result was exactly the same as if I had ignited a smudge pot. My son sped over from his house five miles away to save me from possibly fatal smoke inhalation. After that he drove over every morning and tended the fire himself.

I would like to tell you I behaved heroically during the power outage, but this was not the case. The best I could do was to keep my candles burning.

I did meet heroic people, though. These saviors were utility workers dressed in heavy clothes and hard hats and boots. They brought chain saws and huge spools of cable. Many of them worked aloft in cherry pickers during the storm. Suddenly my electric lights were burning. Power restored!

Communication Skills

It is no doubt because of my advanced age that I tend to view more and more things with alarm. Lately, I have been dismayed by the lack of hand-writing skills possessed by many of the young people I encounter. One of my grandsons mails me cherished thank you notes which are always hand-printed on a pretty card. I asked him if he ever uses cursive writing. He replied that he does not, explaining that his only class in cursive writing had been long ago, when he was in the third grade, and he has never tried it since. He and his contemporaries communicate primarily by e-mail, text-messaging, and now, twittering. "But," he informed me proudly, "I know how to read cursive writing."

"Well!" I thought, "that is certainly is a minimal requirement for status as a literate person." But at the same time, I was touched when I realized that his sending me a card through the postal system was something he did especially for me out of respect for my old-fashioned ways.

Following this, I had another eye-opener. While my great-grandson was undergoing the rigors of boot camp in Georgia, I mailed him encouraging hand-written notes from time to time, only to discover that he couldn't decipher what I had written. I was astounded, since my handwriting is perfectly legible to all the people I write to who are age thirty-five or older. But, as his mother pointed out to me, he perceives cursive writing as a foreign language!

Evidently the communication gap between the old and the young is widening so rapidly that it may become unbridgeable. However, I decided to make an effort. So I sat down at my old, slow computer which I use for three purposes: word-processing, a limited amount of e-mailing, and research on the internet. I asked Google to please explain twittering to me.

Google referred me to Wikipedia which has a lot to say on the subject. "Twittering is a free social networking and blogging service that enables its users to send messages known as tweets." Tweets, it tells me, consist of 140 characters, and ingenuity is required to conform to this rigid format. The method commonly used to make the message fit the allotted space is a procrustean process of truncating words by eliminating many letters, mostly vowels. The recipient of the message must then retrofit the missing vowels and consonants to decipher the message. Wikipedia has a long list of tweets, a vocabulary understood only by guesswork and by certain abbreviations which have gained common acceptance. LOL, for example has come to mean "lots of laughs", GF stands for "girl friend", although depending on context, I suppose it could also mean God Forbid.

Twittering, I learned, was developed by a man named Jack Dorsey. He and a group of his associates had a brain storming session in order to come up with a catchy name for the marketing of his new product. He states, "We wanted to capture that feeling, the physical sensation that you're buzzing your friend's pocket." The name "Twitch" was discarded as not creating the "right imagery." Twitter was chosen because its dictionary definition exactly describes the product: "a short burst of inconsequential information." Another possible name comes to mind—"twaddle," but I suppose that doesn't create the right imagery either. It certainly would not do to have one's friends "twaddling" in one's pocket.

I cannot overcome the feeling that twittering wastes a great deal of time accomplishing something which is almost meaningless. Why, I wonder, should we embrace a technology that encourages us to go skimming through life like water bugs on a pond.

As you may have guessed, my research on twittering has done nothing to ease my mind. I now have a horrifying vision of millions of mostly young people sending inconsequential information in all directions to other people who must then reconstitute vapid messages by tediously inserting letters here and there. The reconstituting process reminds me of adding water to the MRE's (Meals Ready To Eat), the barely palatable food packets issued to soldiers in the field. Twittering adds nothing of value to anybody's intellectual menu as far as I can tell.

If one wants to employ a language short on vowels, why not study the Czech language? One could then send (or perhaps even *write* in flowing script on scented stationery!) a whole lot of interesting, possibly romantic messages, to any Bohemian of one's acquaintance.

For The Moment

The maple tree in my front yard, presented to me eight years ago as an eightieth birthday gift from my daughter and one of her friends, is so beautiful in its autumn array that I want to spray it with some kind of fixative, like the one women use to keep their hair in place. The tree is covered with leaves in all shades of yellow and coral and it glows in a glory that surely cannot be replicated. I don't want a single leaf to fall. My mind formulates a heart-felt but foolish wish: "Oh, please don't let this beauty fade away. Let nothing change! I have seen perfection. It is enough!" But I know, even as my mind composes a kind of psalm, that the leaves will soon be swept away. Only a short reprieve is possible. It is a day of intermittent sunshine and light showers. So far the rain drops are small and sparse, and there is no wind; the leaves will remain undisturbed just a little longer before they are beaten off the branches by a fiercer rain or they are swirled skyward by gusting winds. I seek to comfort myself by thinking that this lovely spectacle will appear again next year. Yet my heart tells me to hold onto this moment. A familiar pesky demon reminds me that I may not be here next year, and that even if I am, conditions may not then or ever repeat a sight as flawless as the one I see right now. I remember a line from J.L Carr's *A Month in the Country*, "We can ask and ask, but we can't ever have again what we once thought was ours forever." We acknowledge the transient nature of beauty and the impermanence of delight with the utmost reluctance.

Perhaps that is why a certain kind of miserliness sometimes accompanies old age. In our late decades we may become desperate to retain what we have, because we are all too aware of how much has already slipped away. It is a time of life that is marked by what one person described as "a series of amputations." This is a bald and drastic statement of the losses that are inescapable for anyone who lives a long time. Personally I prefer the poetic line from *The Last Rose of Summer* which says "When from love's shining circle the gems drop away." But no matter how you express it, the truth is that life must eventually resolve into a pattern of down-sizing, adjustment, compromise and diminished expectations. Either we learn to savor

each day's gifts without greedily demanding the impossible of
tomorrow, or else we become very mean-spirited indeed and are
scowling old people whose bitterness shrivels everyone around us.

While I have been pondering these weighty matters, it has
grown dark, but I think I will put on a sweater and go out into the yard
with my high-powered flashlight to take another look at the maple tree.
I will be very careful as I go down the porch steps.

Pull Yourself Together

Any time I encounter a boxed item that comes with the words, "some assembly required," I have an immediate sinking spell. Last week I opened a package containing the components for an elaborate telephone which my kindly audiologist ordered for me when she fitted me with hearing aids. This is a sophisticated instrument available free of charge to anyone with a hearing disability. Enclosed was a paper with an 800 number to call for help in assembly and installation. As it happens, automated telephone calls are also high on my list of unnerving experiences which I make every effort to avoid. There was zero likelihood of my being able to reconstruct a telephone by means of automated instruction, even if the voice giving directions was programmed to sound like benevolent old Alexander Graham Bell himself.

Fortunately I have a son who has been taking things apart and putting them back together since he was two years old. When I called him he said hastily, "Now don't touch a thing, Mom, I'll come right over and set it up for you." (He long ago learned that any attempt by me to become technically or mechanically self-reliant inevitably ends in a pile of rubble.)

In a matter of minutes, he had my splendid phone ready to perform innumerable functions I had not heretofore realized I needed: call waiting, call forwarding, date and time of day, answering machine, a menu of frequently called numbers, volume control, and flashing lights to alert me to an incoming call in case the ringer is not set at an optimal loudness level. It also has dual lighted number panels, and the hand set can be worn on a cord around the neck or the system can be used with headphones. Needless to say, there are miscellaneous large and small buttons, aside from the numbers, which activate various functions. For sheer versatility, this phone is the electronic equivalent of a super-deluxe Swiss army knife.

"I tell you what, Mom, I'm a little short on time today," my son said, "but I'll come over tomorrow morning and we'll go over the manual together so you'll know exactly how everything works. You don't need to fiddle around with it today."

71

Unfortunately he did not reckon with the Pandora Factor in my nature; I sometimes have the urge to tamper with things which are far better left alone. After he departed, I carried my old (1990's) telephone to the bedroom where it replaced an even older (1980's) model, which I placed in my bag of items to take to the thrift store. Then I returned to the kitchen to admire my state of the art new model.

Surely there would be no harm in seeing if the thing was actually working. I lifted the hand set and pressed the "talk" button. Yes, there was a robust sounding dial tone. Then I noted two large buttons with on and off labels. I pressed the off button and was informed by an unemotional voice that I had entered "off." I pressed the on button and was told I had entered "on." My goodness, how simple could the whole thing be! Then I pressed a tiny button with a wee label I could not exactly discern without my glasses.

It was at this point that the entire telephone suddenly lit up with a startling display of spectacularly flashing red lights, exactly like a juke box, except that it was ominously silent. In a panic, I pressed the off button and was informed I had entered off; nevertheless, the lurid display pulsated on unabated. I tried pushing all the other buttons, one after the other, but the instrument, like Edgar Allen Poe's relentless "Telltale Heart," continued throbbing. So, despite my terror of electrocution, or some other grisly type of death by science, I gingerly unplugged the phone. The display continued without skipping a beat.

"Oh, help!" I cried, in case there were any friendly deities loitering about. There being none, I was forced to the solution of last resort. It was up to me to remove the two sets of batteries that were the phone's remaining power source. When I accomplished this, the lights went out, and I sank, trembling, into the nearest chair.

The next day, after a meaningful sidelong glance at me, my son reassembled the phone. "Well," he said, "I guess it won't do any harm if we take a look at the instructions in the manual."

The Opera Fan

My eight year old great-grandson, Dillon, responded to music as soon as he could wiggle, and became a dedicated percussionist at age two when he discovered how to beat a stick against the top of an empty oatmeal box and an over-turned tin can. By the time he was three, he began vocalizing the tunes he heard. He seemed particularly pleased with the acoustics in his grandmother's barn where he spent a lot of time during his pre-school years warbling away like an oriole during mating season. Since I am perilously close to being a-musical and cannot carry a tune to save my life, his innate musicality appeared to me to be an absolute miracle.

Dillon's grandmother, my daughter, Barbara, fortunately did not take after me. She is a devotee of classical music, particularly of grand opera. As you would expect, she has been overjoyed that her one and only grandchild is a music lover, too. When the Metropolitan Opera presented a simulcast of Hansel and Gretel a couple of years ago, she took Dillon to his first opera. He was enthralled.

The next year when the schedule of the Metropolitan simulcasts was released, there did not seem to be any performance exactly suitable for a young child, but because Dillon was so enthused about going to another opera, his grandmother checked the list again and decided Lucia Di Lammermoor would appeal to him from a musical standpoint. The admittedly hair-raising plot, she rationalized, is actually no more violent than that of his favorite movie, Star Wars. Lucia would perhaps be all right for him if she went over the story ahead of time and he understood what to expect.

He therefore knew that the heroine, Lucia, had been hoodwinked by her unscrupulous brother into believing that her true love, Edgardo, had betrayed her. On top of that her no-good brother then inveigled her into signing a marriage contract with a rich man she did not love. Furthermore, Edgardo, although he tried hard, did not arrive on the scene in time to prevent her marriage. This combination of stressful events naturally drove Lucia crazy so that she was not really herself when she stabbed her new bridegroom to death.

On opera day, Dillon, who has a strong sense of occasion, arrived dressed in his black suit, complete with vest, white shirt and necktie. (He particularly likes this outfit because he thinks it makes him look like his adored grandpa, who wears a three-piece suit when he goes to his office.)

I awaited the outcome of the whole venture with a great deal of trepidation because I clearly remembered going to Joan Sutherland's performance of Lucia with my late husband. It was so electrifyingly intense that I found myself gripping the arms of my seat for fear I might levitate.

I needn't have feared for Dillon's safety, however. When I asked Barbara how he had done, she replied, "He just loved it. He was rooting for Lucia all the way."

"But," she added, "Have you ever tried to have a discussion about women's rights with an eight year old boy? He absolutely couldn't figure out why Lucia should have to marry someone she didn't want to. He told me his mother wouldn't have put up with a thing like that for five minutes!"

Dillon later saw "Daughter of the Regiment," which he thought was all right, but he declared that "Lucia" was, no question, his all-time favorite opera.

Last week Dillon announced he had made a decision about who he wanted to be for Halloween: "This year I'm going to be Lucia."

An eerie vision of the mad scene from Lucia flashed into my mind. Watching a wild-haired soprano in a blood-soaked night gown, hitting all the high notes as she descends a long staircase after having just committed a murder, tends to linger in one's memory. I could well imagine that Dillon must have decided that in this guise, Lucia was the spookiest figure anybody might ever expect to encounter.

His mother and grandmother explained to Dillon that, apart from seasoned opera-goers like himself, Lucia is not generally so very well known; other people might not recognize who he is supposed to be. At present he is leaning toward dressing as Darth Vader.

Dillon and his grandmother are scheduled to attend Aida and Tales of Hoffman this year. Who knows what the outcome may be.

Old Ladies Having Tea

One of the great pleasures of my retirement years has been the opportunity for leisurely conversations with my contemporaries while we have a cup of tea together. For us, truly, "the time has come to speak of many things." I have discovered that all of us are amazed that a lifetime has passed so swiftly and that we are, to our astonishment, old ladies. One of my friends who lately turned ninety exclaimed, "How did this happen!" And to our considerable dismay, the pace of life has continued to accelerate!

Since we grew up in an era which idealized "gracious living," when we meet, we still want our guests to know that their presence is a special occasion for us. We try to "set a pretty table." We bring out our lace table cloths and dainty embroidered napkins and arrange bouquets of flowers. We are apt to drink our tea out of fragile heirloom china cups and we serve delicate cookies baked especially for the occasion. In this sense, we are reliving a part of our past and undoubtedly appear anachronistic in a world of fast foods, plastic containers and canned soda pop. And yes, we do reminisce, but usually this is for purposes of comparing what life used to be like as contrasted with what life is for us today.

Although we laughingly concede that we appear to be quaint and out of touch, a surprising number of us have learned to utilize computers for word processing, to e-mail our families and friends on a daily basis and to seek information on the internet. On the other hand, we voice our deep resentment over being forced to use implacable and impersonal automated telephones systems; we resist paying our bills electronically because we feel the personal control of our affairs is slipping away from us; and we share horror stories about the near impossibility of obtaining human help when we are lost and desperate in the entanglement created whenever our technology goes awry.

We express our concern for our children and our grandchildren whose frantic schedules seem to mirror the high speed connections that technology offers us. This is undoubtedly a valuable capability in some applications, but surely not one to be adopted as a total life style. We have wondered if any scientists are trying to build introspection into their technology. It seems to many of us that there is less and less consideration of nuances of meaning, of allowing for the "maybe" and the "perhaps" aspects of life. Can programs for compassion and moral conviction be down-loaded into a computer?

When we are told that there is the likelihood of technology out-stripping human intelligence, we nod our heads in agreement. I am certainly obliged to acknowledge that in my case, this occurred quite a while ago. More than once I have said to my computer, "Okay, you win. Have your own way! Now just exactly what is it you want me to do?"

A recent topic discussed among us has been the newspaper and magazine articles reporting the possibility in the near future of a hostile takeover of society by robots infected with evil intentions. This, we are told is no longer in the realm of science fiction. One elderly lady's response to this piece of news was, "Well, I guess there are some advantages to being old. Maybe we'll all be lucky enough to die before that happens! Please pass the cookies."

Tea parties have been prominent in the news lately as a form of social protest inspired by the Boston tea party of our country's early revolutionary days. The type of tea party I have been talking about, though, is the kind that used to be reported on the society page of newspapers. On that account it may perhaps be regarded as a frivolous, even insignificant way, to spend one's time. I beg to differ.

Old ladies having tea together get right down to the nitty-gritties of life. We will insist on the value of being human and the power of love until we drop the last lump of sugar into our cup. We know exactly what A.E. Housman meant when he wrote: "Take my hand quick and tell me,/ What have you in your heart."

Looking Back: Remembering the Great Gifts of Old Age

As we "older people" wend our way through our eighties and into our nineties, we are exhorted to fight old age tooth and nail. We are particularly admonished against living in the past. We are urged to be in the present, to look ahead, to change with the times.

The main problem with this advice is that we have spent a whole lifetime building our past and we are the products of it. This is not something we can jettison very easily, nor should we want to. One of the great gifts of old age is the leisure to remember and consider the background that formed us and possibly to share this information with those who are following after us. Perhaps our lives can be thought of as a reconnaissance mission. In a sense we have scouted the territory and can report on conditions.

Additionally, we have had time to sort through the successes and failures of our lives, to reflect on what worked in our human journey and what did not. We may have grown strong enough to combine self-inspection and retrospection and forgive ourselves for our wrong turns and mistakes in judgment. This entails forgiving others, too, and tends to make us more compassionate.

I believe we are often less rigid in our judgments in old age than in our youth because we have discovered that there are always more questions about the serious problems of life than there are answers. Quite often there is no perfect answer. There are countless variables and unknowns in every equation one encounters and frequently there turns out to be more than one possible solution.

We have concluded that there are always "circumstances beyond our control." Times change, but history, although often reinterpreted, does not. As our lives move forward, it is well to take a backward glance occasionally and even pause to visit the archives. There is much helpful information stored there by our predecessors

When we indulge ourselves in nostalgia, it is to revisit the people, places and events that brought us joy. These "sentimental journeys" are certainly good for us and there is comfort in these

77

remembrances. Sometimes though, when we acknowledge the bitter and tragic hours of our lives, we offer breathing proof that life with all its sorrows is still worth living. A remark I heard long ago lingers in my memory. "One thing that attests to the goodness of life is the great sadness those who are old feel over the death of someone who is young." The most important legacy the old may leave to the young is the simple reassurance that life is a gift, precious beyond price.

Contrary to the belief that old age is a time when all passions are spent, it is more likely to be a time when we care most deeply, even desperately, about everything from our most fundamental personal relationships to the global course of human events. We know that our individual actions matter and can affect others in profound and often unsuspected ways.

If we sometimes rail against "progress," it is not, as a rule, because we are too hide-bound to accept change but because we have discovered that progress always comes with a price. We certainly have the wit to acknowledge that technological advances have brought enormous benefits to every aspect of our lives, but at the same time we are all too aware that technology enables us to kill each other more effectively at both close and long range, that the pace of life has been accelerated and complicated to a point that verges on hysteria, and that simple personal contact is more and more often bypassed in favor of instant messaging. We are distressed when efficiency trumps humanity.

When we elderly people are urged to "get with the program," our tendency is to say, "Well, now wait a minute while I think this over." The difficulty is that we are no longer allowed minutes to weigh and consider matters — only nano-seconds. During our late years we are apt to feel as if we are being hustled through life like Japanese commuters being pushed forcibly onto high-speed public transit.

The scene around us often has a fragmented, shifting, disturbingly kaleidoscopic aspect. At this point we may ask, "What's the rush?" Two lines written almost a century ago by W.H. Davies, an English poet, come to mind. "What is this life if full of care/ We have no time to stand and stare."

I'm Not Leaving Right Away

Whenever I encounter friends of my own age whom I haven't had an opportunity to see for a while, their conversation is likely to begin with three questions: "Are you in good health?" "Are you still in your own home?" "Are you still driving?"

The answer to these questions is "Yes, Yes and Yes." And to myself I say, "So far, so good!" because I often feel like a high wire artist trying not to look down as I negotiate a dare-devil crossing over Niagara Falls.

Any of us in our late eighties who have been lucky enough to retain our common sense and are still able to manage our personal affairs at least well enough to remain solvent and avoid arrest, know that our lives are more and more fraught with "life-altering circumstances." There is a point, perhaps not far distant, when certain wrenching decisions may have to be made. If we are lucky, we make these decisions for ourselves; otherwise we may end up with other people, who love us and honestly do "have our best interests at heart," forced to make decisions for us.

I think of a friend who stopped by for his daily visit with his mother, age 83, only to find her walking about on the roof of her house checking out her rain gutters. After assisting her back down to earth, and reminding her that he would gladly have attended to the gutters himself, he confiscated her ladder.

There are many instances of cars being towed away or keys being hidden from aged parents who insist upon driving even when their driving skills have deteriorated to the point where they are a danger to themselves and to others. The role reversal of becoming "the parent of my parents," as one person expressed it, is a time of heart-ache (and sometimes of out-right war) for all concerned. Perhaps the saddest thing the offspring of elderly parents ever do is to assume the management of their lives. I look at my daughter and son who have had a lifetime of studying my peculiarities and who sometimes understand me better than I understand myself, and I am thankful they both have a good sense of humor. They may need it.

Relinquishment is the hardest lesson of old age. The fierce desire to retain autonomy is apt to skew our judgment and may prevent us from knowing "when to hold and when to fold." Our reasoning may be further clouded by our hoping the oft-quoted statement that the eighties are now the new sixties may be true. Perhaps if we just have the right attitude and eat a healthy diet, we can still be hale and hearty and out plowing the south forty for at least another decade.

While it is statistically true that as a general population we are living longer and healthier lives than previous generations, that still does not alter the fact that each of us seems to be stamped with a personal "Use by" date. Longevity, good health, and sustained mental acuity are primarily determined, so scientists concede, by a combination of good fortune and a favorable genetic endowment. But these too have their limits.

What I am talking about here are the thoughts that tend to occupy my mind at two o'clock in the morning, when, like a great many other old people, I am wakeful after having made my second or third trip to the bathroom. With deep regret, I must tell you that despite my nocturnal ponderings, I have not arrived at any perfectly satisfactory resolution of a single one of the problems of aging. I am tempted to go into my Scarlett O'Hara mode and decide to think about all this tomorrow, except that a glance at the clock tells me it already is tomorrow.

Perhaps the best strategy for dealing with old age lies in developing a saintly attitude so as to accept with grace whatever befalls us. On the other hand I read a research study a while back that indicated that cranky people in nursing homes tend to live longer than the kind and undemanding ones. So much for sweetness and light!

As of this morning, I am feeling quite lively. Yes, I can be reached at my usual address; and yes, I am still driving with utmost caution around the local area. Reckless as it may be, I have decided to continue buying my weekly supply of green bananas.

Paradox of Age: Looking Older, Feeling Young

It stands to reason that by the time you have reached your mid-80s, you may have had to undergo some overhaul and repair, not to mention a replacement of parts. You're going to have some cherished contemporaries who have an assortment of things wrong with them. At this time of life, I notice we inquire after each other's health somewhat diffidently.

"Um, you're looking fine, are you feeling OK?"

Last week, when a friend who has been dealing with a series of health problems called from Southern California, I nerved myself to inquire how she was doing.

"Well, I'm seeing every kind of doctor but an obstetrician," she replied with a laugh. Then she went on to tell me about a long trip she is planning to take next month with a favorite travel partner and after that described the wonderful cruise they enjoyed last spring. Apparently during the intervals she spends at home, she allots whatever she considers a reasonable amount of time for various specialists to do their probing and testing and then away she goes again to have a good time.

For many years I have carried on an alternate-month correspondence with a Cheyenne high school classmate who lives in Laramie, Wyo. We have not seen each other since 1940. Of course, we both know we are "little old ladies," but I still picture her as "Miss Frontier," the queen of Cheyenne's famous Frontier Days rodeo, and I suppose I still appear in her mind's eye as young and reasonably fair. There is something to be said about this kind of relationship.

One of Oscar Wilde's witticisms was, "The tragedy of old age is not that one is old, but that one is young." This is the paradox of aging: outward appearances often belie how one feels on the inside.

When my friend and I write to each other, we discuss our feelings about everything from arthritis to widowhood to retirement homes, acknowledging that these are facts of life for us, but any melancholy is removed because we are, after all, still young girls together.

81

We go on to speak of books and family and all the things that make us happy. I describe my garden and give her the details of my grandson's wedding. She tells me of cross-country skiing with a group of seniors and admits she feels silly and kind of guilty over having recently purchased a small SUV. I tell her I hope the SUV is a red one.

The Southern California friend mentioned earlier once told me, "I don't mind getting old, but I do mind getting ugly! Just look at all these lines and age spots!" I was taken by surprise because I consider her very attractive, and I was privately marveling at her vitality and intelligence. I took her age spots for granted just as I accept my own most of the time.

However, sometimes one is jolted into awareness of the ravages of time by such things as the unblinking stare of a great-grandchild who remarks, "You're awfully old, aren't you, Grandma?" or the over-solicitous young hostess who does everything but follow you about with a wheelchair in case you might be going to have a sinking spell. There is no way to explain in these circumstances that, although you appear rickety, desiccated and pre-historic, and may actually at that very moment be experiencing mild indigestion plus a certain amount of chronic join pain, you are still enjoying life immensely and are terribly pleased to be around. There is no point, either, in quoting Oscar Wilde.

It is true that many old people are prepared to respond with a detailed inventory of body parts when someone asks how they feel. They are like the old gentleman who, when asked how he was, replied, "Well, my head aches, my elbow is stiff, my back is sore and my feet hurt. And to tell you the truth, *I* don't feel so good either." There is a temptation to dwell upon a long list of fascinating infirmities and to compare scars. The complaints are legitimate.

On the other hand, it is equally true that when some elderly persons with multiple health problems say, "I feel fine!" they are speaking honestly, too. Their reply is from that contradictory inner self that dismisses outward appearances. They are still welcoming life's possibilities, no matter how limited they may be. Quite often there is a smile, and even a hint of mischief, in their eyes.

Change of Status

Last week, completely without warning, I became the family matriarch. This is a weighty designation with implications of royalty. The job description includes a variety of ceremonial duties one may or may not feel up to performing. Queen Victoria, the quintessential matriarch, found the whole business so overwhelming she became reclusive. As a sovereign she was publicly venerated, and people did a lot of tugging at their forelocks when she was around, but privately she was considered a real grouch for not showing up at each and every public function.

On the other hand, the late Queen Mum was a much softer matriarchal model. You will remember what a hard-working lady *she* was! She wore a perpetual smile, and there was never a minute when she wasn't waving at somebody. Still, since she was always surrounded by lackeys who anticipated her every need, acting benign in that kind of set-up ought to be fairly easy.

Aside from being an old woman, I bear no resemblance to either Queen Victoria or the Queen Mum. Furthermore, I have never felt comfortable in the limelight. The suddenness of my elevation from plain grandma to matriarch, found me ill-prepared. When I left my quiet pastoral life in the hill country and flew down to Southern California for my grandson's wedding, I had no intention of being an active participant in this splendid affair.

Then I was told that as the eldest female member of our family, it was my responsibility to lead the entire wedding procession down the aisle! This involved a major deployment of personnel. I was to be followed by the bride's mother, ushered to her seat by her son; then the mother of the groom, then two adorable small children, the flower girl and the ring-bearer; and close on their heels, nine resplendent, satin-sheathed bridesmaids escorted by nine stalwart ushers in tail coats; followed by the gorgeous bride on the arm of her father. It occurred to me that in an onslaught of this magnitude, the casualties are always highest in the vanguard. Of *course* I was nervous!

Nevertheless, at a cue from the wedding coordinator, I took my son's arm and did my best version of a stately walk down the church's fifteen mile long middle aisle while under the avid scrutiny of 300 guests. Although I suddenly developed a tic under my right eye, I assumed what I hoped was a gracious expression. Perhaps I looked majestic. Let us hope.

During the festivities following the ceremony, I was cosseted in the style befitting a dignitary of my stature. A coterie of attentive people asked if I was warm enough, was I able to walk up the stairs to the reception, or did I need to take the elevator, did I want another glass of champagne (actually, I had to restrain my usual impulse to leap up and start waiting on other people), was my seat comfortable, could I hear the bride's father's welcoming speech to the guests, was the sumptuous dinner satisfactory, was the music too loud for my taste?

Back home in the hills, I am by no means neglected, but I do lead a fairly self-sufficient life. I scurry up and down the stairs in my home a dozen times a day. I do my own shopping for groceries and make a point of propelling the shopping cart instead of employing it as a walker, as I've noticed many elderly people tend to do. If I want a second glass of anything, I fetch it for myself. I regulate the volume on the T-V to suit my aging ears, and make myself comfortable on whatever chair is near by. I pump my own gasoline and personally carry out my trash barrels every week. However, now that I am the august female head of my clan, all this must change. I will perforce have to leave the mundane matters of daily living to whichever of my minions are idling about. I will need to concentrate on acting venerable and constantly remember that I am an old woman with considerable clout. Henceforth our family conclaves will be governed by my imperial hand, but, *noblesse oblige*, I will do a certain amount of waving, too.

I Need Help

Like many other retirees who have ample time for a thorough reading of the morning paper, I scan the obituaries to ascertain that my name is not featured, and then turn to the police and sheriff's blotters, still published in our local newspaper, to check on whatever mischief my fellow-citizens have been up to in the last twenty-four hours.

There appears to be no limit to bizarre incidents and no bounds to human eccentricity. It is understandable that people calling in to report strange or illegal activities, or to request help in domestic upheavals or neighborhood vendettas, are so often incapable of giving a coherent account of what is going on. For most of us, calling for assistance from law enforcement is a desperate measure, resorted to only when our problems seem so extreme we cannot cope with them on our own. Under this kind of duress it's no wonder that we may blurt out long-hidden family secrets or make odd, non-sequitur comments which, when quoted in print, are often mirth-provoking.

Fortunately my one and only call to the sheriffs department, made a couple of years ago, was never officially published. What happened was this: I looked out my front window one summer evening and beheld a llama making its stately way up the middle of the street. A full-grown llama on the loose in my quiet little residential area is not anything one would ever expect to see. I recognized an emergency when I saw one.

I keep a list of emergency numbers posted on my refrigerator door. The present situation did not seem to me exactly like a 911 emergency, but, as I scanned the list, the sheriff's department looked like the best agency to call.

Taking my phone with me, I stood on the front porch where I could keep an eye on the llama and punched in the sheriff's number. When the dispatcher answered, I said "I'm calling because there's a lla---"

"Give me you name please." I complied.

"There's a llam----"

."Address please." I complied

"There's a lla----"

85

"Telephone number?" I complied.

"There's llama walking down, or maybe it's up, my cul-de-sac!" (I have a directional problem.)

"A llama?"

"Yes, an animal llama spelled with two l's, not a religious lama spelled with just one."

"I understand."

I felt compelled to impress upon the dispatcher that this was an absolutely unique event. "This llama is treading where no llama has ever trod before!"

"Our department is not really equipped to handle---"

"Oh, my gosh!" I shouted into the phone, "The llama is being followed by a herd of goats!" For, at that moment, six or eight goats of assorted sizes and colors appeared from behind the eleagnus hedge bordering my property. The lead goat was wearing a bell which tinkled merrily. "They're all gamboling about and nibbling on my eleagnus!"

"Um---I'm sorry, but we're not really equipped to handle this kind of problem. You need to contact animal control."

"Animal control? Oh, yes. They're on my list."

My son, who had been working on something in the garage, alerted by the sound of the bell, stepped outside to check on what was going on. He took one look at the procession of animals and shouted, "I'll run down to the corner and head them off before they get out into traffic."

As he raced away, another man, also running at top speed, emerged from a driveway at the end of the cul-de-sac. "The electric fence got turned off," he yelled to me as he passed.

I was still mystified, but since two grown men had taken charge of matters, I decided it was up to them to call for help if they needed it. The llama appeared serene, which is more than I can say for myself, and the goats were enjoying themselves with the total abandon of revelers in a Mardi Gras parade.

You, I'm sure, immediately figured out that the animals were escapees from a brushing company. But at that time I had never heard of using goats, complete with a guardian llama, to clear land. Our neighbor had contracted to have the vacant lot adjacent to his house cleared, preparatory to planting a garden. The owner of the goats, called by the neighbor's wife, arrived in his truck, herded the animals back to their duties and re-activated the electric fence.

Who knows what the dispatcher thought. I'm lucky I was not referred to the mental health department.

The Gift of Time

There are a couple of things that most of us who are elderly really resent. We hate being ignored and we cringe at being patronized. Many of us who are over eighty have had the experience of attending social functions among younger people where we seemed to be not merely over-looked, but totally invisible. Conversely, we have been in situations where we have been hovered over and cosseted by altruistic types who feel duty-bound to compliment us on "still being so alert."

Both of these situations are hurtful because in the first instance we are not recognized as people who are apt to have anything interesting to contribute to a conversation, and in the second instance we are verbally patted on the head as if we have, against all expectations, managed to say something intelligent.

When we are conducting business or legal transactions, particularly if we are women, we often realize that we are regarded as poor old dears who are probably not mentally competent. If we are accompanied to an appointment by anyone younger than we are, we are apt to become mere by-standers in a discussion, as all remarks and explanations are directed, over our heads, to the younger person. I am, admittedly, a scuffed- looking old lady, but I am lucid, and sometimes I have wanted to wave and call out, "Yoo-hoo, it's my business we're discussing here and I still have command of my faculties, so talk to me!" Some of my contemporaries have expressed such a sense of outrage over this kind of treatment that only the fear of having an attack of apoplexy has restrained them from whacking the offender with their purse in the style of the feisty lady on the old "Laugh-In" show.

It often seems to me that in our society, old age is regarded as a tragedy, and the elderly are too quickly categorized as pitiful and depressed and likely to be out of touch with reality. This is sometimes true, of course, but it is not universally true and should not be assumed as a given.

Old age is simply a stage of our lives, and, yes, perhaps the most difficult one of all. It is a time fraught with anxieties and marked by radical changes in our lifestyle, and we are required to learn the hard lessons of relinquishment and down-sizing, but most of us who are lucky enough to be living through it are still delighted to be here. We cherish our families and our friendships because we have learned how precious they are and because we know that the most innocent of partings can be a final good-bye. We savor life. We recognize laughter as the best medicine for us and find humor in the predicaments and aggravations of our daily lives.

Many of us seek out reading and discussion groups. We read with a greater depth of understanding, and perhaps we listen with heightened respect to the opinions of others, although we also feel more free (or even obligated) to disagree with what we perceive as outrageous.

At a recent study group, I was reminded once again of the writings of Carl Jung, whose insights I have always admired. One of his theories was that human beings live into old age for a specific reason. The old, he said, have wisdom to impart and they are the vehicles for the transmission of culture from one generation to the next. When I mentioned this to the group, we all had a hearty laugh, because one of the standing jokes among us who are old is that we are absolutely brimming with good advice nobody wants to hear.

It occurs to me that perhaps a more aggressive marketing of our skills is needed. One modest way to begin might be a tasteful ad in our local newspaper:

LIMITED TIME OFFER: Free-lance oracle with 85 years experience now offering 24-hour a day service at no charge to caller. Patience and understanding guaranteed. No appointment necessary. Bonus lecture included with every consultation. Call toll-free number 800---------. TIME IS OF THE ESSENCE! ACT NOW!

Oh, Say, Can You See?

A recent addition to my ever-lengthening list of anxieties is my serious concern about how our national anthem is now being sung. It is no longer The Star-Spangled Banner, but the Star-Mangled Banner, or as a friend of mine suggested, The Star-Strangled Banner. To my aging ears, it has lately lost its heart-lifting quality and instead sounds profoundly disheartening. It has become a lament.

Before every major sporting event, it seems some well-known and, one hopes, well-meaning rock star makes his or her way to the microphone. This person is inevitably wearing sexy, oh boy! look- at-me, show-biz type clothing composed of glitter and spandex, and for night time affairs is bathed in a light display which rivals the aurora borealis. What follows is an a cappella rendition of our national anthem in which no single note is ever hit squarely. There is a wavering, ululating quality about the whole performance. If one understands and appreciates soul music, (and as you've surmised, I probably do not) the performance may be a tour de force and may even be comparable to the late Luciano Pavarotti hitting three or four operatic high C's in a row. However I can't help a feeling of incongruity. The soul of the anthem seems to me to be destroyed by the very singer who is attempting to project that exact quality.

I yearn to hear it sung by a stout-hearted baritone, someone like the long gone Nelson Eddy, for instance, who would make every note ring clear and true and in the process lift our self-confidence to heroic levels. And, alas, Kate Smith is no longer with us either. An imposing and no-nonsense soprano of her caliber would likewise be able to inspire in us a sense of pride and gratitude for our American heritage

Ah, and then I remember when we all used to sing the anthem ourselves at whatever event we were attending. In this low-budget version of life, we stood in a grandstand or auditorium with our hands over our hearts and did our level best to sing what is admittedly a difficult song for the average person. Even if we didn't come within half an octave of hitting the sustained high note, we would have given it our best try, and as a bonus would experience the goose-pimply feeling of being united in some spiritual way with all the people singing around us.

An anthem is defined as a song of praise or celebration. Any sensible person is going to have to acknowledge that praiseworthy and celebratory material is presently in short supply. When we are surrounded by every conceivable type of human discord augmented by a worldwide avalanche of natural disasters, it is easier to relate to mournful songs like "Bury Me Not On the Lone Prairie." or "Nobody Knows the Trouble I See," There seems far more to howl about than to cheer about. Yet this is exactly the time for a powerful, ringing reminder that courage is what is required "for the living of these days."

Our national anthem was never intended to be a dirge. It has a heroic motif and above all it now asks a challenging question: "Does the star-spangled banner yet wave o'er the land of the free and the home of the brave?"

No quavering or self-pitying answer will do.

The Movie Goer

Movie special effects have simply gotten out of hand. Lately, while attending two or three blockbuster movies in a row, I have felt like a victim of assault and battery. To begin with, Dolby surround sound is jolting enough to destroy brain tissue, and prolonged exposure to it must certainly result in acoustic trauma. Secondly, putting on 3D glasses becomes the prelude to experiencing a kind of guided missile attack. The movie theater becomes a war zone. When I have dared to look around, I have expected to see dead bodies lying in the aisles. And I wonder if the next innovation will be to install explosive devices under the theater seats.

I am one of a trio of little old ladies who look forward to enjoying lunch together, and then attending an afternoon matinee. Of late, we have attended some highly rated, three or four- star movies, and have emerged from the theater feeling lucky to have survived. Then we ask each other, "Now exactly what was that whole thing about?"

As long-time movie fans, we are certainly not averse to innovation and excitement. We buy tickets because we want to be fascinated, enriched, amused or entertained and above all to become involved in what we're looking at. What we do not want is "sound and fury signifying nothing."

It used to be that film stars were the ones who carried a movie. Sometimes their sheer glamour or force of personality could make the ordinary seem wonderful, poignant, sinister or funny. They were the main attraction. They may have been seriously flawed people in real life, but on screen they embodied the ideal. The acting of the great stars left us a legacy of splendid and memorable performances.

However, it seems to me that in present day films, the stars may become mere adjuncts to spectacular special effects which are undoubtedly impressive as purely technical achievements but do little to enrich the plot or augment our understanding of the motivations of the characters.

Of course old-time movies were padded with some simple special effects, too. (Hours of dialog are hard to write!).Early on, the

93

familiar car chase, which is still with us, became routine in any action movie. However in olden days it was merely a short diversion and although it might end in a crash, it was never grisly in the sense of having severed body parts flying through the air.

The first time I ever saw anything akin to a car chase was in a "picture show" I attended eighty years ago (the word "movie" may not yet have been invented!). I forget the title of this opus, but I know it starred the Oklahoma humorist, Will Rogers, paired with a timid comedienne named Zazu Pitts. Her talent lay in her sad-sack portrayals of characters who were the blameless victims of life, lost souls absolutely resigned to suffering every conceivable kind of mischance.

In the scene I remember, these two simple, lovable characters are in an open touring sedan, free-wheeling down a steep, one-way mountain road. He is valiantly trying to steer the run-away car around hair pin turns as their speed relentlessly accelerates. She is haplessly hanging on to her hat, caught as usual, in circumstances beyond her control, with no happy ending in sight.

The sequence was scary but at the same time hilarious. Furthermore, what the actors seemed to be experiencing was something the audience could relate to. We saw the actors as people just like us. We were riding along with them; the outcome concerned all of us. Probably that is why this scene has lingered in my memory and still makes me smile when I think about it.

As I get older, one of the matters I tend to ponder is the possibility that human beings may become redundant in an automated and technologically sophisticated world. Scientists are now seriously discussing the matter of singularity which as I understand it is the real possibility that technology (robots?) could turn on us and eventually usurp control of our lives. Can it be that my concern over this prospect has morphed into a neurosis? Am I crazy to worry about cinema special effects producing "reel" people who are not "real" people anymore?

Like Zazu Pitts, maybe the only thing I can do is just hang onto my hat and await developments, hair-raising though they may be.

Rhyme and Reason

There is certainly no shortage of advice for the elderly, and I can testify that most of us welcome thoughtful suggestions or helpful hints, especially the ones from our grandchildren about how to make our computers work. At this time of life we are not about to sneer at guardian angels. Being watched over is comforting since it suggests that there are those who still want us to stick around.

But along with the positive advice of family, friends, our doctor(s), dentist, gerontologist and the AARP, we are also deluged with unsolicited brochures and catalogs offering solutions to any age-related problem (including death) that could possibly arise.

For example, my mail box on any given day, may contain a letter urging me to check into a reverse mortgage at once in order to ensure myself of a stable income for the rest of my life; a special invitation to an investment seminar, with limited seating, which will tell me not only how to protect my income, but actually augment it; a warning that I may not be aware of the full extent of my hearing loss and should take advantage of the enclosed offer of a free hearing test by a qualified specialist; a notice from my insurance company stating that my house is now nearly forty years old and should be re-wired and re-plumbed to forestall a significant rise in my insurance rates; and a thoughtfully worded letter and brochure from a mortuary pointing out that it's the responsibility of a considerate person like me to have a pre-paid funeral plan which will protect my family from having to make final arrangements for me at a time when they may be emotionally upset.

In addition, technology has identified me as being in the demographic group most likely to pay attention to catalogs advertising orthopedic shoes, elastic stockings, shoulder braces, and moisture-proof bed pads. Such publications are replete with pseudo-reassuring pictures of smiling white-haired people using clever assistive devices. These range from relatively inexpensive long-handled pincers which enable one to retrieve items from high shelves and clamps for unscrewing jar lids, to very expensive walk-in bath tubs, stairway elevators and a variety of motorized conveyances designed for both indoor and outdoor use.

I tell you, there are times when it takes a stout heart and a firm grip on reality to enable me to sort through my mail. Even so, a certain amount of depression is inevitable.

One way of coping with this is to engage in a stern inner dialog. I remind myself that sometimes a person can be given too much advice; one must learn to be selective. None of my current crop of problems is unmanageable. There is no point in conjuring up the most terrifying "what ifs" of life, especially when one is pretty imaginative to begin with.

After this no-nonsense conversation with myself, I seek out a soft and cozy place where I can prop up one of my heavy-weight poetry anthologies. Poetry has always been a comfort to me. Shakespeare, Longfellow, Wordsworth, Emily Dickinson and Robert Frost have seen me through some rough places in my life. So have Lewis Carroll, Ogden Nash and Dr. Seuss.

To my surprise, it turns out that what I thought was my own private antidote for anxiety is one shared by others. Not long ago I read a small book entitled *The Merry Heart*. This is a compilation of speeches given by the late Canadian author, Robertson Davies, when he was in his eighties. When this distinguished and compassionate man was pressed for the best advice he could offer to the elderly, he responded: Study poetry.

Grow old along with me!
The best is yet to be,
The last of life, for which the first was made:
Our times are in his hand
Who saith: "a whole I planned,
Youth shows but half; trust God, see all, nor be afraid."
by Robert Browning

As the Twig is Bent

In these times when there is a global selection of adoptable children, I often speculate on the combination of nature and nurture as it applies to the polyglot population of transplanted young ones. This is unquestionably a complex subject that provides endless study for sociologists and psychologists. It is also an area of personal interest to me because at age three, I was placed in the Wyoming State Children's Home along with my three older brothers. In 1924 we became wards of the Commission of Child and Animal Protection.

Unlikely as it may seem, we came from what was, to us, a happy home. Our family structure had been demolished by the death of our mother the previous year. Our father, whom we adored, was a teamster and ranch hand whose hard-won earnings were all too often diluted by bootleg whiskey. As a widower, with no extended family and few resources, he found himself incapable of caring for us and somehow made arrangements for us to be taken into the orphanage. He agreed to pay the state of Wyoming forty dollars a month to care for the four of us. He left us there with a promise to return for us. But he never did, nor did he ever pay the State.

All I remember about him is that I held his index finger as I walked into the orphanage office, proud and protected by his great size. I still relive the feeling of his finger slipping from my grasp, as he walked away.

Although we were not grossly mistreated, I was placed in a girls' building separate from the brothers I had worshiped and depended upon all my life. I caught glimpses of them at mealtimes sitting at a table with a group of boys when all the children assembled in a large dining room, but I was never allowed to be with them. The four of us soon understood that there was some stigma attached to being "home kids," and that custodial care was strict and impersonal, and that our idiosyncrasies were punishable offenses.

Within a year, I suppose because our father had defaulted on his payments, each of us was parceled out to a different family in widely separated towns in Wyoming. The woman who was supposed to become my new mother, became seriously ill and I was returned to the orphanage, by long train trips, not once, but three times, as her health went through successive stages of improvement and deterioration.

After my third return I was taken for a week-end visit to my seven year old brother at his new home in Cheyenne. We greeted each other like the long-lost relatives we actually were.

My brother who surmised I was there on a trial basis, hovered over me all day long, shared his new toys with me and kept telling me how nice his new mother and daddy treated him. He made absolutely sure I did everything just right, and even combed my hair and washed my face before dinner so I would make a favorable impression.

As we snuggled together in bed that night, he decided to leave nothing to chance. He instructed me to go out into the living room and tell his new parents that I wanted to be their little girl. Naturally I was afraid to do this, but he insisted, and since I figured it was a good idea to obey just about everybody, I tiptoed down the hall and delivered the message verbatim.

By an overnight miracle, my brother and I were once again united. (Some years later we reconnected with our older brothers when they came to Cheyenne to live.)

We were cared for and loved, for better or for worse, by two extraordinary parents whom we came to love with all our hearts. Surely they have been given special accommodations in heaven, for they shared with us everything they had and never once mentioned the sacrifices they made on our behalf

Still, had I not been raised with my brother, I would never have known exactly who I was. Happy as we were in our new life, we still shared a private sense of "otherness," and held to a tenuous thread of our beginnings. I believe this duality must exist, perhaps at some subliminal level, in the many adopted children today who face far more radical and complex adjustments than my brother and I ever did.

May these children grow and thrive!

Basic Needs

During his 1928 presidential campaign Herbert Hoover himself never actually uttered the words "a chicken in every pot and an automobile in every back yard," but the Republican Party did run ads proclaiming that this would be what people could expect if he was elected. As campaign promises go, this now sounds modest enough, but the words rang hollow during the Great Depression that blighted Hoover's presidency and shook the economic foundations of the country. Daily bread and shoes without holes were hard enough to come by, let alone stewing chickens and automobiles.

In contrast, it is interesting to consider what we are now programmed to believe is essential to our survival. Present day basics require: two motor vehicles in every garage, immediate and unlimited access to a supply of Kentucky Fried Chicken, a boat and/or motor home under a tarpaulin in the side yard, at least one high-speed, late model computer, a telephone in every room, plus individual cell phones for each family member, and multiple television sets to accommodate the tastes of varying age groups.

Those of us who were children in the 1920's and thirties remember we were always "saving up" for something. In this we emulated our mothers who had a sugar bowl or a canning jar where they deposited small change, so as to have a little money on hand for "emergencies," not that every day didn't present an emergency of some kind. Every one of us children had little banks where we deposited pennies and nickels and even the occasional dime a grandparent might give us for meritorious service beyond the call of duty. We estimated our wealth by the weight of our banks which we shook daily to enjoy the music of tinkling coins. We were small misers in training because withdrawals were frowned upon. Instant gratification was a concept yet to be invented.

Recently when I was with a gathering of elderly friends, the talk turned to a review of the homes we grew up in. Some of us described weather-beaten ranch cabins, or solitary farm homes, and others spoke of spacious houses in attractive neighborhoods. But no matter what the family's circumstances were, our recollection was that change came slowly. Even when the times gradually improved our parents remained conservative, cautious, if not actually tight-fisted with money. Innovations were weighed and tested.

Most of us recalled the momentous day when the first telephone was installed in our house. When it rang, it was always startling, almost like receiving an electrical shock. The fleetest family member available was dispatched to rush upstairs or downstairs or all the way across the house to answer it with a breathless "hello." The telephone was strictly non-portable and of course there was no answering machine to take a message. A missed call left the whole family speculating fretfully about who in the world the caller might have been.

One person remarked, "We had a nice big two-storey house and a large family, but there was just one bathroom." It then occurred to the rest of us that, although we now automatically take it for granted that any house being built must have at least two bathrooms, we, too, had grown up in a house with a single bathroom. (A couple of people remembered no bathrooms at all---just out-houses.)

Oddly enough, none of us could recall any particular difficulty sharing a bathroom. I can remember chatting companionably with my mother while I took a bath and she brushed her teeth. When my brother combed his hair in the morning, he routinely shared the medicine cabinet mirror with our father who was lathering up for a shave. If we had overnight guests, and we frequently did, the family got up earlier than usual to use the bathroom. We children understood that we must not dawdle about in the bathroom and that family honor depended upon our leaving it in immaculate condition for company.

As usual when comparing the distant and slower paced past with the demanding and feverish present, it is easy to cast a rosy aura around our yesterdays. However, history always reminds us that "untroubled times" are actually non-existent.

My fervent hope is that today's children will someday look back on our present depression and social upheaval and recall it with a smile as a time when they and their parents made the best of things as they actually were, while they simultaneously tried to make the world a better place.

Rating System

Late in his life, my husband, who was a thoughtful and also a sometimes whimsical man, one day announced, "I've concluded that I am just a utility model human being. I would very much like to have been a deluxe model or even a sports model, but that simply is not the case, I'm a utility model and that's all there is to it."

My response was to laugh, because what flashed through my mind were automobiles that fit into each of these categories, and I instantly tried to match him to one of them.

The first mental picture I had was of a massive vehicle once owned by some friends, a 1950's era, top of the line Cadillac, shining with chrome, and sporting large tail fins. Over-voluptuous it certainly was, but in its day it represented luxury and affluence. My husband was right; he definitely did not fit into that category. Wretched excess was not his thing.

The sports car I envisioned was a gull wing Maserati we had seen years ago in front of a restaurant in Santa Barbara. When the sides of this amazing vehicle majestically lifted up and two splendid-looking people emerged, I remember a feeling as surreal as if I were looking at alien creatures disembarking from a space craft. No again. My husband was a down to earth kind of fellow. Though he enjoyed novelty and inspected this unique car with delight, he would never have considered it his alter ego.

And then there was my Uncle Ted's quintessentially utilitarian Model T Ford, dull black, of course, which unfalteringly carried him every single day for years on end to his job at the wholesale grocery warehouse. Hmmm, well, yes, my husband, being half Swedish, was wonderfully systematic and dependable and he also possessed the same kind of endurance as Henry Ford's all but immortal car; but against this, was the jaunty Bohemian half of his heritage which required, color and music and innovation and complexity to keep life interesting. No, he definitely was not a Model T type.

"Listen," I said, "you are in a class all by yourself, probably some kind of custom-built hybrid, but whatever you are, I have

101

absolutely no intention of trading you in for some flashy new model. You still rank pretty high in customer satisfaction."

Sometimes self-evaluation can be a pitiless thing. We in the geriatric population are, I think, prone to be especially hard on ourselves when we look back, because we know that we have not accomplished all that we set out to do in life. People of our generation were likely to have been indoctrinated in Latin class with the heroic maxim *Ad aspera per astra* which roughly translates: reaching the stars through great difficulties. Many of us, as children, witnessed our parents doing exactly that as they struggled to give us the best life possible during the depths of the Great Depression. We were, in a sense, programmed to set lofty goals for ourselves, to leave behind us "footprints in the sands of time."

We older people were fortunate in that so many of our working years were spent during a long period of prosperity. This was a time when many of our dreams actually did come true, and against all reason lured us into supposing that by working just a little bit harder we could meet any goal we had set for ourselves.

The most damning thing that could be said of anyone was, "He sure didn't amount to much." So, we aspired to making our mark in life, and it didn't occur to us that there was an absolute limit to how many of us could become president of the United States.

Come to think of it, my husband might have made a really great president. He was raised on a dry farm in Colorado where the whole family worked endless hours to eke out a bare living. The children in that family were admonished to: "Make yourself useful instead of ornamental." Since that became the guiding principle of his life, it's no wonder he concluded that he was "just a utility model human being." Serviceable is a far better designation. He gave a great deal and he wore well. And he also touched the stars.

Laughing All The Way

Recently an elderly couple struggling to figure out how to use their new laptop computer ended up clowning and making faces at it as an antidote to their confusion and frustration in coping with yet another technological mystery. They did not realize they were being recorded until their granddaughter picked up on their hi-jinks and thought they were so funny she put them on YouTube. To the couple's astonishment, they became immediate YouTube stars.

Older viewers probably felt an immediate kinship with the couple. They recognized the gallantry of people who could laugh in the face of adversity and thereby diminish its power. Younger viewers on the other hand may have been amazed that old people could act so silly and have so much fun. The fact is that a robust sense of humor (or a sense of the ridiculous) is what enables many of us to live with the mounting technological challenges we face in our old age. My impression is that the stress level for the elderly rises in direct proportion to the number of new electronic marvels marketed every year.

I remember my white-haired aunt used to say, "Just when you think you're going to make ends meet, somebody moves an end." In our present circumstances, this could be paraphrased to "Just when you begin to understand your big old desk-top computer, somebody gives you the latest thousand application device that you can't use at all."

The industry's tendency to miniaturize their products to the size of a cigarette package is but another complication in the life of older people. It means that the first step in using such a device is to remember where we last laid it down. This may consume as much as half a day. Telephones can now be carried almost anyplace, and most households may have several lying randomly about. I have sometimes waited around for one of them to ring and then if my hearing aids are working properly and the phone has not somehow slipped behind the sofa cushions, I am finally able to localize its position. (I loved those old telephones that stayed put and had well-defined ear pieces and mouth pieces. You knew immediately where they were and which end to talk into and which end to listen to.)

Another thing that challenges the capabilities of some of us is that so many devices look alike. I don't know about you, but I have more than once tried to make a telephone call on my t-v remote control doohickey. This is unsettling even when you are alone, but if a young and heretofore admiring great-grandchild witnesses your error, you feel that you've plummeted several levels in his esteem. When he politely hands you the proper instrument, all you can do is thank him, adjust your ego and your bifocals, and try to remember who it was you intended to call.

Manual dexterity, like everything else, certainly deteriorates with age. Therefore, it should surprise nobody that grandpa and grandma may lack precision when using a touch pad or a keyboard or when pressing the miniscule symbols on some ultra compact device. My fingers now seem to me much larger than they used to be and are not suitable for delicate maneuvers. As I see it, if you make one wrong move, or over-lap just the least bit, you can be a goner. Yes, I know that in the right hands our electronic servants are supposed to be forgiving and eager to correct any error. This has not been my experience; apparently I always do something completely unforgivable.

Although we are "strangers and afraid in a world we never made," as A.E. Housman would have put it, I note with pride that my generation is gallantly struggling to adapt to existing conditions. Some are making the transition into cyber-world with remarkable skill and grace. For others of us it is an unrelenting battle which we try to relieve with jokes and comic antics, rather like school children who find class-work beyond their capabilities and compensate by becoming the class clowns.

I once heard a minister remark that he planned to preach a sermon on a new beatitude. He would entitle it, "Blessed are the silly for they shall gladden our hearts." No wonder the couple on YouTube were so well-received.

Changing Tempo

Long ago when I, a musically untalented child, struggled through the piano lessons my gifted mother had been denied, I was introduced to the frantically fast tempo of the tarantella. My music teacher, who always sought to make our sessions interesting, explained that the tarantella depicts the frenzied dance by which, in olden times, victims of a spider bite tried to ward off death. This gruesome bit of information enlivened my music lesson that day, of course, and has stayed in my memory for over eighty years.

However, if my music teacher supposed that knowing the history of the tarantella could somehow inspire me to play faster than was required for the barcarolles and minuets I had heretofore belabored, she soon had to accept that this was not going to happen. At best my tarantella always sounded quite a bit like the Song of the Volga Boatmen. I had already reached the outermost limits of my digital speed and manual dexterity.

I now find myself in somewhat the same predicament with regard to modern technology. In order to survive in this present world I have learned to use a computer for basic functions such as word processing, searching the internet for information and sending and receiving e-mail. I cautiously press as few buttons as possible to achieve my objectives, having found that any experimentation or teensy deviation from the simple steps I have learned results in my having to hire someone at $65.00 per hour to correct whatever unimaginable cybernetic havoc I have wrought.

Although I now have accepted my limitations and achieved a somewhat uncertain control over my computer output, I am helpless to stem the incoming tide of computer generated and highly detailed printed statements that fill my mail box every month. Without exception, these statements inform me that I could take care of practically all of my business affairs by simply going on line. This sounds as hazardous to me as going out on a limb. Evidently I am some kind of control freak, but I really do like to have an understanding of what I'm doing. I know computers in general, and my computer in particular, are far smarter than I am and much, much

105

faster. Once again I have had to acknowledge that I am still playing a minuet in a tarantella tempo world.

Furthermore, I feel deprived of the right to move at my own speed through the dignified and serene old age I had anticipated. I once believed I could live out my retirement years in tranquility. My imagination painted a picture no doubt influenced by long ago Disney movies and Norman Rockwell Saturday Evening Post covers. I saw myself, silver-haired and benign, settled comfortably in a rocking chair shelling peas or paring apples. The reality is that I am a harassed and grumpy old lady hunched over my desk pawing through menacing stacks of documents which I eventually transfer to ever-fattening files. I am afraid to throw anything away and my income tax preparer turns pale when I show up with my yearly records. (I have even gone so far as to retrieve torn up documents from my waste basket and scotch tape them together again lest I might have inadvertently discarded something fiscally significant.)

When I mentioned my frustrations to one of my contemporaries not long ago, she looked at me with a knowing smile. "I understand exactly what you mean," she said. "I solved the problem by hiring a young stay-at-home-mom who previously worked as an accountant. She charges me a reasonable rate to come in an hour or two twice a month to keep my household and business affairs straight. She goes over everything with me in a way I can understand and then all I do is write out the checks and sign them. I figure the peace of mind is worth what I pay her. I economize somewhere else."

I have the young woman's telephone number close at hand. I am wondering if I, too, might find peace by hiring her to do what she is fully competent to do, while I relax and enjoy the soothing tempo of a comfortable rocking chair.

I am still very good at paring apples and shelling peas.

Introduction to Politics

Growing up in Cheyenne, Wyoming, the capital city of the least populated state in the Union, had some distinct advantages. Even as a small child in the 1920's I knew that we lived in the biggest and most important city in the state, and that our gold-domed capitol building was one any state would be proud of. A huge World War I canon on the front lawn stood as a symbol of power and might. My older brother, Floyd, and I spent a lot of time on the capitol grounds because he had discovered that the broad sidewalks surrounding the stately building were the smoothest and best sidewalks in town for roller skating.

The city park was adjacent to the capitol grounds and sometimes on the days our mother had a bridge party to go to, we were allowed to pack a peanut butter sandwich, a cookie or two and a banana into a paper sack and have our own private lunch there in the shade of the big cottonwood trees.

The governor frequently walked through the park going to and from his lunch at the governor's mansion which was a few blocks away. We noticed that the elderly retired gentlemen who sat on the green park benches reminiscing about the early days when Cheyenne was just a cow town, or shaking their heads over the death of some of Cheyenne's most promising young men in the trenches in France just a few years back, always called out "Good morning , governor." as he passed. Some of them called to him by his first name because they had known him and his family for years. His response was always cordial, and often he stopped and chatted for a while, leaving the old men smiling as he took his leave.

Floyd and I exchanged greetings with the governor, too. We had made his acquaintance one day when we ventured inside the capitol doors. It was my brother's idea to go in and have a look around, although I was petrified at being some place where I thought we ought not to be. Fortunately I was evidently born with a strong heart because I did not faint dead away when a door labeled Office of the Governor, opened and out walked the governor himself.

"Well hello there," he said. "Are you two looking for somebody?"

Floyd, as usual, was self possessed, and answered truthfully that we weren't looking for anybody but just wanted to see inside. As we stood in the rotunda, the governor pointed in one direction and told us the state representatives met in chambers there, and then pointed in the opposite direction toward the wing of the building where the senate met. "Too bad the legislature isn't in session," he said, "but go ahead and have a look anyway. Then you'll know where our laws are made."

"Thank you," Floyd responded politely, "but I was wondering if we could go up in the dome and look around." I was horrified at his audacity and wanted to "sink through the floor with embarrassment," as our mother would have put it.

"Well why not," the governor laughed, obviously amused that he was dealing with a youngster who had high aspirations.

And so it was that Floyd and I walked around inside the capitol dome in Cheyenne, Wyoming, gazing through each and every small window at the full panoramic view of a city that was beautiful in our eyes.

Later in the year we returned to the capitol building when the legislature was in session. We watched from the gallery as laws were being presented by state senators and representatives who shouted and argued and pounded their fists on their desks and then took the votes that determined the fate of Wyoming's vast resources. We wondered why law-makers were so quarrelsome and then often ended up slapping each other on the back or shaking hands in a friendly manner before leaving the chamber together. It was our introduction into the complexities and seeming contradictions of democratic government.

Floyd probably cast his first vote in Wyoming, but my first vote was in California because I turned twenty-one here shortly after my marriage.

I have voted in every election since then, still wondering why law makers are so very quarrelsome.

My Word

Ten years ago, when I turned eighty, I began writing essays. I have no recollection of exactly why I did this. Perhaps it was the need to have something to contribute to the writing group I attended, or maybe it was because I thought I had a few things I really wanted to say. I even purchased a splendid new electric typewriter on which I painstakingly tapped out these short pieces. But because I am not a good typist to begin with, I still ended up with the same kind of battered and contused manuscripts I had produced with my massive old Underwood which was second hand when my father gave it to me in 1935. The writing group begged me to learn to use a word processor.

Although we had a computer in the house because my son had been given one as a gift when he was making a long and tedious recovery from surgery, I had no intention of ever going near the thing. I still entertained the illusion that I could live a peaceful old age by ignoring the technological revolution altogether.

However, a very dear friend, who explained that she had always "just loved gadgets" gladly embraced the electronic age in her retirement and quickly became computer literate. (Her brother was an IBM executive so she probably had a genetic predisposition for this sort of thing.). She volunteered to give my son some computer tutorials, and she urged me to sit in on their daily sessions. Out of politeness, I sat across the room from them part of the time. But my heart and mind were always on the book I had just been reading, or out in the garden, or up in the kitchen. I nodded off from time to time.

The insidious thing that happened, though, is that technical words and phrases began to seep into my consciousness. I was being converted to technology by osmosis!

As my son progressed through playing solitaire to e-mailing, to surfing the net, to filing and storing information, and to writing letters with a word processor that instantly allowed him to revise sentences and correct spelling errors with a mere tap here and there, it dawned on me that a computer is not an entirely bad thing. You will be amazed to hear that it has taken me only a decade to learn to do the things I have just mentioned.

Sadly, one of the truths about technology is that there are no plateaus where a person can settle down and relax for a while. It is not enough to be able to e-mail family and friends and communicate in complete sentences, and share pictures or informative or humorous articles with them. It is now imperative that one be on Facebook connected to thousands of known and unknown people who are designated as your friends. Some of them think nothing of using obscene language or perhaps sending you the latest nude photograph of themselves. Responses we receive to a simple statement we may have posted will more than likely be something on the order of "Right on!" Or "Man, you really hit it!" Or "Oh, oh, somebody's cranky today." This kind of thing begins to sound like, "Me Tarzan You Jane," language reduced to little better than the positive and negative grunts of primitive man.

Having a Wonderful Time

My self-willed Jack Russell terrier, Wrigley, seemed to laugh to himself all the way through obedience class. Accepting orders from anybody was a concept he found too far-fetched to consider. He danced about, watching the other dogs in the class agreeing to sit, heel, and come to their owners on command, but he, personally, or perhaps I should say, doggedly, resisted knuckling under in any way.

The instructor took one look at Wrigley and commented, "Sometimes these terriers can be piss-ants." Yes, indeed! When we emerged from training, I was bloody, so to speak, and Wrigley was unbowed. Wrigley and I were allowed to appear in the picture of the graduating class, but this was merely a courtesy, extended because I had paid a fee for the course.

Wrigley was my 75th birthday present from my daughter, Barbara, who had heard me remark that I considered Jack Russell's "just adorable." Well, they are, and the small black and white puppy I received certainly was. He was also hyperkinetic. Although he was so toy-like that people's first impulse upon seeing him was to cuddle him, they immediately learned that he had needle sharp teeth and claws and had no desire to snuggle up to anybody. He was capable of more escape movements than a hooked trout. Even my vet was surprised at his resistance to being held. That is why I named him Wrigley.

My assumption was that as Wrigley matured he would slow down and gradually become more attentive to me. What actually happened was that as he grew, he developed hair-trigger reflexes, and a compact and beautifully muscled body built for speed. He was therefore better equipped than ever to dodge my out-stretched hand and to whiz off in the opposite direction whenever I called him. He was almost untouchable unless he decided it was time to play, in which case he dropped his ball at my feet and impatiently allowed me to pat his head a couple of times. He was civil at meal-time, but never demeaned himself by begging and could not be lured into compliance by the offer of a dog biscuit.

The miracle is that he did accept a leash. My only explanation for this is that he knew it indicated a change of scene, and therefore

111

offered the possibility of adventure, or better yet---escape, for he became an incorrigible run-away. The lure of the great beyond was irresistible to him. On leash, he could scarcely wait to turn the next corner.

On the occasion when he managed to slip his leash, I spent an entire afternoon, assisted by a posse of compassionate friends, trying to round him up. He stayed within our neighborhood and frequent sightings of him were reported; but, as usual, he would not come when he was called and gaily skittered away as soon as anyone came within ten feet of him. Then he vanished. At dusk, the search was suspended. I drove home exhausted, frustrated and heart-sick. Exasperating as he was, I did love Wrigley. I tried not to think of him as a broken little terrier, lying suffering and alone in some ditch beside the road.

I needn't have worried. He was on the front steps waiting for me. He showed no remorse whatsoever, and was unmoved by my gladsome cries. He condescended to accept the two pats on his head which were his set limit for receiving affection. Here was a creature whose theme song had to be *I Did It My Way*.

Now that Wrigley had discovered the joys of running free, containing him became a major issue. If the doorbell rang, he charged the door, not for the purpose of greeting anybody, but in order to be in position to streak through the merest crack when the door began to open. Anyone visiting me was treated to the sounds of a scuffle as I grabbed his harness and struggled to hold him back with one hand while opening the door with the other hand. If he made good his escape, I was faced with yet another anguished waiting period until he trotted home in his own good time.

As my friends watched the mounting strain of my efforts to co-exist with Wrigley, they began to make such comments as, "My goodness, that dog is a full-time career," or, (more bluntly) "At your age, you shouldn't even be trying to cope with an animal as active as that!" All of this was too true.

When Wrigley began to dig his way out of my fenced back yard on a routine basis, my daughter said, "Mom, getting Wrigley for you was a big mistake. He's got his own mission in life. It includes more action than you can ever give him. Would you be willing to part with him if I can find a good home for him?" I was so weary I was beyond protesting, but I couldn't imagine who in the world would take him.

Yet within a week of beginning her search, Barbara was contacted by a kindly retired gentleman named Al, who lived on four fenced acres with his two enormous mixed-breed dogs. He had always wanted a Jack Russell terrier, he said, because he admired their spirited nature. Boy, did we ever have a terrier answering *that* description!

When we took Wrigley for a get-acquainted visit, I was aghast at the size of the two dogs who met us at the gate baying out a basso profundo duet that sounded like something from Russian opera. Either dog appeared capable of swallowing Wrigley whole without so much as a follow-up burp.

"Come on in!" Al shouted as he opened the gate for us, "they won't hurt you-they're as gentle as lambs." Wrigley, on a leash, charged forward in his usual head-long fashion and found himself at nose to fore-leg level with one of these hairy behemoths.

The baying abruptly ceased as two massive muzzles lowered in unison to sniff over the wee morsel suddenly at their disposal. I stopped breathing altogether. Wrigley became a statue. And then, amazingly, two massive rumps rose up in unison, giving the universal canine signal for "let's play!" Wrigley responded in kind, his stumpy tail vibrating with enthusiasm.

"You might as well take his leash off and let him have some fun," Al said. What ensued was a kind of impromptu canine ballet. Wrigley danced lightly around his new friends, then, with an inviting glance at them, whirled off across the landscape like a small dust devil. The huge dogs, taken by surprise, took a moment to gather themselves to lumber after him. Wrigley led the heavy-footed duo in an ever-widening circle, weaving intricate patterns between and around them. For good measure he threw in a few Nijinski style leaps directly in front of them. He was starting to perfect his pirouettes when they panted to a halt in exhaustion.

"Now that's what I call action!" Al exclaimed. "What a wonderful dog!"

Then he called, "Wrigley, come here, boy!" And Wrigley *came*! He seemed to smile companionably as Al patted him on the head five or six times.

Al sent us a Christmas card along with a snapshot showing Wrigley sitting regally at ease on a couch, with the two big dogs lying on the floor looking worshipfully up at him. If Wrigley had been able to append a note, it likely would have read, "Having a wonderful time. Too bad you're not here."

Nessie

At age eighty, and against my better judgment, I fell deeply in love with an amiable Scottish gentleman. He was debonair, obliging and intelligent, but, alas, already committed to a long-term relationship.

I could only ask, "Are there any more at home like you?"

His mistress laughed, and I think Andy did, too. West Highland Terriers do seem to have a sense of humor.

"I can put you in touch with Janet, Andy's breeder," she said.

"Oh, no," I said, suddenly coming to my senses, "I'd be crazy to get a puppy at my age."

"You wouldn't necessarily need to get a puppy. Janet's a member of a Scottish dog rescue organization. They're always looking for good homes for older or 'special' dogs."

So, yes, I called Janet. She asked what age dog I had in mind and which sex I preferred.

"A male," I said, picturing Andy, "around four or five years old – I understand Westies are long-lived dogs." I didn't want my dog to outlive me and become someone else's responsibility.

Janet called back within two weeks. "I may have just the dog for you. She's a sweet little female her breeder intended to show, but she's had a medical problem."

"Um, what sort of medical problem?"

"It's a condition that sometimes occurs in terriers. Blood circulation to the hip is insufficient, and the hip bones deteriorate."

"Uh, how bad is this exactly?" I remembered seeing a picture of a dachshund who had been fitted out with a set of wheels after his rear end had failed.

"The affected bone tissue has been removed, and she's developed compensatory muscular support. She's made an excellent recovery."

"Ah, erm," I hedged, "you say it's a female - I thought a male dog might relate better to me. How old is she?"

"Twenty-one months. She's very well-trained. Just from talking to you, I somehow feel a female dog is right for you."

115

I was doing some quick calculating as we talked. "I'm eighty years old "my thoughts ran, "and Westies often live to be twelve or fourteen. Subtract twenty-one months from that expected life-span, and that equals ten to twelve years. Add that to my age, and it means I'll have to reach at least ninety-two to out-live the dog."

Janet was in a waiting mode on the other end of the line.

"When can I see her?" I blurted recklessly. A week later, Janet and her fellow-breeder, Chuck, arrived on my doorstep. He carried a tote bag which he set on the window seat in my kitchen.

"Oh, you didn't bring the dog with you," I said, trying to hide my disappointment so as not to seem over-eager.

"She's right there in the carrier," Chuck replied, pointing to the bag. I then noted that the sides of the bag were mesh and that it was indeed a pet carrier. But there was no sound from within and no detectable movement.

"Is she all right!" I exclaimed. It occurred to me that she might have expired during transit.

"Oh, Candy's fine. She's used to being transported. I'll let her out in a few minutes when we look over your yard." He and Janet were giving my home and yard the kind of scrutiny that a couple of top sergeants might give to a barracks.

At this juncture my son, Russ, who lives with me when he is not away traveling on his job, walked in the door. I introduced him to Janet and Chuck- "the rescue people I've been telling you about."

"Hmmm," Chuck said. "I didn't know anybody else lived with you. That might make a difference in Candy's bonding process."

"She'll bond to Russ right away," I replied confidently. There has never been a dog yet who has not become starry-eyed upon meeting Russ.

"That's what I mean," he said.

It dawned on me that he thought Candy might become attached to my son instead of me. "I'm sure she'll relate well to both of us. And I will be the primary care giver." I wanted Chuck to know that when it comes to bonding, I am a person with Velcro-like qualities.

"Why don't we let Candy out in the yard so you can look her over, and we can check the fences?" Janet suggested.

I led the way onto my back deck, where Chuck at last opened the carrier. Out stepped a perfectly calm, immaculately groomed, self-assured little white dog with prick ears, obsidian black eyes and a matching black nose. She looked about her with the non-committal air of a hotel guest checking the accommodations. Then, with the utmost serenity, she peed. With another glance around, she trotted over to the door mat and sat down. She was clearly staking a claim. Bonding had occurred. I now belonged to that dog.

But not so fast! We were still being evaluated. Chuck and Janet pursed their lips over the spacing between the supports of the deck railing and noted the ten-foot drop to the lawn below. They examined the fence and gates for security and pursed their lips again over the height of a retaining wall. They may also have checked for poisonous plants in the flower-beds.

"Good lord," Russ muttered, "do you think we'll have to take a written examination, too?"

Meanwhile, Candy, looking beguilingly beautiful, strolled around the lawn sniffing here and there, occasionally lifting her head to savor the breeze. Her slightly sashaying hip movement only added to her charm. Chuck and Janet reached consensus. In order to make my home acceptable I would have to: 1. enclose the deck with wire to prevent the dog from falling through the uprights, 2. fill in low spots around the bottom of the fence, and 3. enclose the open stairwell they had noticed when they entered my house. Candy would be spayed, they said, and they would bring her back in three weeks for a second visit. Off they went with Candy silent in the carrier.

During the interval, Russ surrounded my entire deck with orchard wire, filled in low spots under the chain link fence with rocks and gravel, and then he and I draped and tied bird netting around the open stair-well.

"You know this is just crazy," he said. "We've never had a suicidal dog yet."

"Furthermore," he groused, "I think 'Candy' is a ridiculous name!"

"What about a Scottish name like Annie or Bonnie?" I suggested.

"Too ordinary. Why don't we call her 'Nessie'? That's as Scottish as you can get."

We did pass muster on the second inspection. Nessie, neé Candy, could dwell with us and be our love. I signed a document transferring ownership from Chuck to me with a clause stating that Nessie was to be returned to Chuck if I became unable to care for her. I was given her complete medical records and a detailed list of instructions about her care and feeding. My first-born child was delivered into my hands with far less guidance.

"Some breeders would have had her put down when the hip problem showed up," Chuck said, giving Nessie a good-bye pat. "But I couldn't do that. My dogs are my family." Janet nodded agreement. She had to get home to care for a sick Scottie she had just rescued from the pound.

"TLC has not vanished from the earth," I thought as they drove away.

As Nessie settled in, we discovered that her hip revision makes it impossible for her to jump up on anything. But she negotiates stairs easily by pushing off with both hind legs at once and she nimbly trots up and down the garden paths, patrolling my yard. Nessie guards our family domain with a gruff "prepare to repel invaders" bark when strangers approach. She greets visitors she knows with a pleased, "Oh goody, we're having company" yap, and she welcomes Russ and me home from even our shortest absences with an impassioned warble. This is some kind of ancient Scottish love song I think.

Several times a day I pick Nessie up and hold her close to my heart, which is where I plan to keep her until I'm at least ninety-two.

In The Style of V. S. Naipaul

Author's note: Believe me, I have no quarrel with V.S.
Naipaul's selection as winner of 2002's Nobel Prize for literature.
(And what a relief that will be to the committee!) However, as a long-
time reader of his, I feel entitled to make a few comments.

In my opinion, reading Naipaul is, as used to be said of holy
matrimony, not to be entered into lightly or unadvisedly. The reader
has got to keep his wits about him when negotiating Naipaul's
leisurely, convoluted and molecularly detailed sentences. Scrupulous
attention to punctuation is an absolute requirement. Although periods
are not a problem, every comma, colon, and semi-colon, as well as
dashes and parentheses must be taken into account. Otherwise, one
arrives at the end of a very long sentence no wiser than when he
began. If he is a conscientious reader, honor will demand he have
another go at it. This is wearying and time-consuming, but I do not
recommend any kind of short-cut such as reading the sentence
backwards. In my experience this is counterproductive if not actually
neurologically hazardous.

After reading Naipaul's autobiographical novel, **The Enigma
of Arrival,** I wondered how it would be to write in the way he does.
One could certainly take one's time, meandering and ruminating at
will, and who could predict what might come to mind? What follows
is my attempt to record a personal experience in the master's style:

My usual practice is to time my visits to Eatmore Supermarket
when the fewest shoppers are apt to be on the premises since I am by
nature a shy and solitary person. My real preference would be to shop
before the store opens for business, but since this is not an option,
12:15 p.m. on Tuesday has become my designated time for marketing,
although this schedule has recently been disrupted by traffic delays
occasioned by the laying of some sort of new pipe line on South
Auburn street which has complicated the lives of the inhabitants of the
modest cottages lining the street, as well as adversely affecting small
businesses in the area, but which is, for me, no more than a minor

annoyance or small inconvenience that I now accept calmly as the price for improvement of the city's infrastructure.

My habit, as I have grown older, is to park my car as close as possible to the compact row of shopping carts near the store entrance so that I have the shortest possible distance to walk across the hot asphalt parking lot which is inevitably littered with candy wrappers, soft drinks cans, discarded cash register receipts and shopping lists. (When I espy the latter among the debris, it gives me occasion to speculate whether the list was lost on the way into the market causing the shopper to forget some vital item such as, say, paprika, which is essential to the preparation of certain dishes---Hungarian goulash, for example.)

Conditions in the parking lot serve as grim reminder of the acedie of a population rendered flabby and careless by a prolonged period of prosperity; and I see around me the signs of the decay of Western civilization.

I proceed with a sigh, thinking of the long-ago hikes I made in my childhood across the Wyoming prairie, where the only trash I encountered was the occasional rusting horseshoe or flattened tobacco can. Time has robbed me of vigor, as it has so many other Eatmore shoppers, and, by will-power alone, I wrest a cart from the snugly fitted row, which at first glance appear to be welded together, hoping that this time I will have, by sheer good fortune, gotten a cart with four perfectly round wheels which will glide smoothly over the recently repaired, but poorly matched, vinyl tile floor with a minimum of effort on my part, and without the clunking and squealing sounds that call attention to my presence as a tired old lady planning to buy a gallon of milk with 1% fat content.

On my most recent visit, when I approached the dairy section, having by-passed the produce section where sprays of water turn on and off at precisely timed intervals, the "on" period being when I have just bent over the lettuce to make a selection from the uniformly round heads now miraculously produced by modern agricultural methods, so that more than once I have had a new hair-do ruined by the unexpected spray and have had to pass, dripping, through the check-out counter to the barely suppressed amusement of the checkers whose reflexes are undoubtedly quicker than mine and who, therefore, have never experience the dousings that I have, as I just mentioned a moment ago, experienced myself, there I became aware of an elderly man , a person whom I never did look at directly, having been trained from earliest childhood to appraise others obliquely by my father who never in his entire life looked anyone squarely in the eye, a man who was methodically picking up the gallon milk jugs one at a time and was sniffing around the yellow cap that sealed each container. I sensed that the man paused as I approached, so, feigning an interest in the bins of dried fruits and nuts nearby, I turned slightly aside in order to give him back his privacy, because he had after all arrived before me, and yet so that I could covertly observe his, to me, extraordinary behavior, since I, personally, had never sniffed a milk jug in my life, nor known anyone else who did.

In order to understand others we must first find some corresponding chord in our own nature, and I searched my mind for recollections of past sniffing activities of my own. I remembered once sniffing at a cantaloupe in the produce section, but it was a discreet, once only, sniff, and I certainly did not sniff at each and every cantaloupe displayed. And of course, there is the kind of sniffing one does upon discovering some forgotten item at the back of one's refrigerator, but that is private sniffing as opposed to the public sniffing I was witnessing.

Perhaps what I was observing was atavistic, the activity of a man who had somehow retained such olfactory acuity that he operated in large measure on his sense of smell rather than relying upon sight and touch alone. Then I reminded myself that the simplest explanation is most likely the true one: perhaps he just liked the scent of milk which may have conjured up the memory of his mother, or even of his grandfather milking a cow in his straw and manure-littered barn in western Nebraska in the late spring of 1927.

There are few avenues I am reluctant to explore, and practically no points I am unwilling to belabor to arrive at what seems to me a logical explanation of events. However, when I noted the gentleman's copious nose hairs glinting in the light from the overhead fluorescent tubes, as he sniffed at and discarded one gallon jug after another, I confess to a revulsion which caused me to abandon my shopping cart and flee from Eatmore Market with such haste that I collided with another elderly lady who was making her laborious way

121

about with a walker, and who stated querulously that if the store was not on fire I should not be in such a hurry.

I have found tinned milk, which I never open without having first washed the top of the container with anti-bacterial soap, an adequate substitute for fresh milk in plastic jugs, but I continue to ponder the enigma of survival in what I now perceive is a frightfully unsanitary world where just anyone at all is free to sniff where he pleases.

Dillon's Wonderful Week

By the time you're six years old, which is exactly what Dillon is, you've already discovered that some days are much better than others. For instance there are days when you don't want to do anything but sing or tap out rhythm on your drums and everybody tells you to "for Pete's sake, be quiet." Or the kid who was your best friend yesterday says, "Get lost!" because he doesn't want to play with you *at all* today. Or there is a peculiar looking thing called a Brussell sprout on your plate at dinner and you have to "just try a bite or two." Or you have to get up early when you're not done sleeping yet, and you have to go to bed when it's not very late at all and you're not even tired. And before you go to bed you have to take a bath.

This week, though, was just about perfect for Dillon. He stayed at his grandma and grandpa's house because his mama and daddy were out of town. Here's what happened to him:

Monday was yard clean-up and gardening day at Dillon's school. Parents and grandparents were invited to come and help with beautifying the grounds. Dillon and his grandma are used to gardening together and he has often helped her attach tubing for her drip system and clean out debris around plants. He knows the difference between flowers and most weeds, plus he has learned to be careful where he steps so that he doesn't squash some brand-new little plant that's just getting started in the world. This requires a lot of paying attention because his grandma is a *very serious* gardener with *millions* of plants.

Anyway, he was glad his grandma was coming to his school; he figured that the two of them could do the best job of anybody. What he did not expect was that when she drove up in her big white truck, which in itself was pretty impressive, she would then unload a beautiful new, dazzling green wagon with John Deere painted on the sides. "I just found this at the hardware store. I thought it would come in handy for hauling away all the old stuff."

The new wagon made the small red wagon he'd had since he was three years old look like a dinky, battered heap. He was lordly as he took possession of this marvelous new equipment. When he realized the other kids' eyes were just about popping out of their heads, he concentrated on looking real cool.

As it turned out, Dillon was right. He and his grandma *did* do the best job and got their area cleaned up in no time. She cautioned him a couple of times not to act "uppity" about sharing his new wagon, but still, he was choosey about exactly who might have a turn with it.

Then, wonder of wonders, as his grandma was leaving, she invited his teacher to come to her house on Friday afternoon and have tea in the garden with them. His teacher was all smiles and said, *yes, she'd just love to come!*

On Tuesday, Dillon went to baseball practice at the park. Everybody on the team of six-year olds was just learning about baseball and mostly they thought the important thing was to know how to slide, so they all slid into bases and slid when they tried to catch a ball or just slid into each other for the fun of it. When they practiced batting and running to first base, the coach had to throw a lot of pitches to every batter before they could finally hit the ball. And then the ball just glanced off the bat and wobbled off a couple of feet in front of the plate while whoever had hit it ran ninety miles an hour to first base and some other kid tried to pick up the ball and throw him out.

When they played their first real game that day and it was Dillon's turn to bat, he decided to bat left-handed. And on the third pitch, he heard and felt for the first time in his life, the unbelievable solid whump of a bat squarely meeting a ball. The ball actually arced through the air toward the mound. The kids all started yelling, "Wow, man, he *hit* it!" And the coach yelled, too. "Run for first! Run for first!"

Dillon looked all around and headed for third base. And his grandma shouted, "No! No! Go the other way!" So he reversed direction and remembered at the last split second to slide and arrived on first base dirty and amazed. All of his team mates were still cheering and jumping up and down.

On Wednesday, Dillon announced to his grandma that he was going to write a story, and he might need some help with the spelling:

The Car
There once was a race car driver, and he
won a race and he was popular. The End.

124

He illustrated the story with drawings of two race cars and then he signed his name which he decided to spell backwards. When his grandma noticed the backwards spelling she said, "Dillon, let me show you something neat." She got a small hand mirror and held the story up in front of it, and said, "Now take a look at your name." Magically the mirror showed his name spelled *forward*! What a marvelous thing to find out about. The kids at school would really be impressed when he explained it to them.

On Thursday, Dillon and his grandma had a conference after school about what to serve when his teacher came for tea. His grandma thought oatmeal cookies would be nice, but Dillon said no he was tired of eating oatmeal and couldn't they have chocolate chip cookies, so that's what they baked and they each sampled one to make sure they had turned out all right. Then they brushed the leaves off the chairs in the gazebo and Dillon wiped off the glass table top with a damp rag. After that, he parked his new green wagon under the near-by weeping beech tree where his teacher would be sure to see it. "I think the wagon looks nice there because it just matches the leaves on the tree."

"Feng shui is very important," his grandma said and explained that feng shui is a Chinese way of arranging everything around you to look and feel just right.

On Friday, Dillon met his teacher at the front gate as soon as she drove up to his grandma's house. "Oh, my goodness, everything looks just beautiful!" his teacher exclaimed as she looked out over the yard where the cherry trees and roses and peonies were blooming. So Dillon and his grandma took her on an escorted tour of the whole yard and Dillon explained to her about the drip system and showed her the rows where corn and peas and beets were planted and the exact spot where the tomatoes would be planted when it was the right time. They had tea in the gazebo with his teacher seated in the best place for viewing his new wagon. When she left she thanked his grandma and him for such a lovely visit, and Dillon and his grandma picked a large bouquet of peonies for her to take with her.

On Saturday Dillon got up very early to take a walk down by the river with his grandpa. And they found a snake! Or maybe the snake found them because it oozed across the path right in front of them and they just about jumped out of their shoes. The snake disappeared into the bushes before Dillon could look at it as long as he wanted to. So his grandpa said they should probably make a visit to the reptile house at the zoo. And that's exactly what they did. Right after breakfast they drove to the zoo in his grandpa's little red car with the top down so that the wind blew their hair in all directions. And Dillon looked carefully at all the snakes in their glassed in compartments. When one of them slid leisurely over and pressed its head against the glass, Dillon pressed a finger on the glass from his side and he looked right into the eyes of the snake. Snakes are very interesting. His grandpa who knows a lot about just about everything said he'd show him a book about snakes and some other reptiles like lizards and alligators.

On Sunday Dillon's grandma fixed big Dutch pancakes for breakfast and he had two helpings of her canned peaches. And then his mama and daddy came back from being away, and there were lots of hugs and kisses and smiles.

Time Travel

Early in the morning just one day prior to my 90th birthday, I found myself whizzing along in an ambulance bound for the hospital emergency room. As I answered the EMT's questions: "Can you tell me your name? What is your address? How long have you lived in Grass Valley? Are you still feeling dizzy?" I was also, oddly enough, remembering a recent telephone conversation with a dear friend who is twenty-five years younger than I am.

"Listen, Lucille, when you turn ninety, don't go anyplace, okay?" she began.

"What do you mean, don't go anyplace? I don't have any trips planned."

"Well you know how older people sometimes set a certain (um) goal for themselves, and then (um) after they (ahem) actually achieve it, they (um) go someplace."

After a mystified few seconds, it dawned on me that she was telling me not to die. "Oh, no, I really want to stick around," I told her in my heartiest tone of voice.

What I did not add was that reaching ninety has been for me a totally impromptu, speed of light excursion through several time warps to an as yet undisclosed destination. Goals! What goals? Also I did not say that at a certain point, birthdays cease being milestones and turn into stumbling blocks.

So I was wheeled into the emergency room, wearing white socks and my least attractive robe and nightgown. My hair was awry and my hearing aids and glasses were at home on the dresser. My son and daughter, both looking very serious, followed me into the curtained cubicle and watched as I made an ungraceful flop from gurney to hospital bed. Both of them had been adamant about calling 911 after my son made his usual early-morning check-up call and I told him I was experiencing an attack of vertigo and was extremely nauseated. (Actually at the time of his call, I was sprawled face down across my kitchen table, clutching at the table edge, praying that the room would stop whirling around me.)

I was certain I recognized what was happening to me because of having just recently read a short article about "benign positional vertigo" which was described as a health problem common among the elderly. At my age I seem to get a lot of health bulletins of various types e-mailed to me by my contemporaries, and I read about maladies I would never have thought of on my own.

The kind and efficient emergency room staff took over immediately, checking blood pressure, listening to my heart, looking into my eyes, palpating here an there, asking questions about what medications I was taking. I tell you, I was as alert as a bird dog, straining to hear every word said to me. I did everything but prick up my ears I wanted so badly to be seen as rational, and fully capable of leading an independent life.

Naturally I announced my self-diagnosis to the staff, but it was clear they were not as impressed and convinced as I had hoped they would be. I was therefore wheeled off for scans of my brain and my heart.

By noon, all testing was complete and had been evaluated. My heart and brain seemed pretty much okay, and the diagnosis arrived at was "benign positional vertigo." I felt it prudent not to say, "That's what I told you in the first place." My dizziness had subsided and I felt ready to go home. However, I was dismayed when the emergency room doctor suggested I should remain hospitalized overnight because of my age. I was so obviously crestfallen that he looked at my son and daughter and asked if there would be anyone able to stay with me overnight in case I had a problem. To my great joy, my son moved one more step closer to saint hood when he volunteered to do this. After being advised to consult with my own physician as promptly as possible, I was wheeled out the door into the sunshine.

I have been referred to a young and very competent occupational therapist skilled in a rapid head-turning maneuver which almost magically relieves the type of vertigo caused by minute debris in the inner ear. Other causes for vertigo I have learned are dehydration and abrupt changes in blood pressure. So, I'm increasing my fluid intake and am also trying to refrain from leaping about in my usual carefree manner.

The Cyber-witch

There was a time when I saw myself as a serene old lady luxuriating in whatever peaceful years of retirement I had left to me. I counted the blessings of good health, a pleasant home of manageable size, a yard with an automatic watering system, a not-quite obsolete TV, assorted middle-aged household appliances, one simple telephone that worked, and a companionable Westie with a life expectancy approximately equal to mine. I was, in other words, lolling about in a fool's paradise.

For years, in my dreamy way, I assumed that technology was something I could take or leave as I saw fit, but as the world around me became more impersonal, more rigidly structured and controlled, I was at last forced to acknowledge that survival depended upon accommodating to a new, yes-or- no, unforgiving technological style of life..

The acquisition of a computer a few years ago marked the end of my easy-going ways. Everyone I knew assured me it would both enrich and simplify my life, plus answer any question I ever had and also put me in instant touch with anyone I need to reach anywhere in the universe.

A platoon of heroic tutors eventually programmed me to interact with my computer to the extent that it now permits me the miracles of e-mail, word processing and internet access. This is far more than I ever aspired to, and it is enough. (I quickly learned that any experimenting on my part with any of a thousand other computer functions ended in disaster.) However Facebook and a blog were established for me, but I do not understand them well enough to use them consistently without eliciting a flurry of snide, pop up warnings stating that whatever it is I think I'm doing is just plain wrong. I am offered any number of http//s claiming to supply helpful connections, but which are actually the entry into a labyrinth from which I can escape an hour or so later only by turning off the computer.

In the course of random clicking in search of guidance, I have noticed and copied down some 800 numbers to be used as a last resort if human assistance is absolutely necessary and all the http://'s have unaccountably been unable to resolve my problem and the computer is notifying me that my problem probably lies with my provider.

I should have known that where my computer is concerned there are no easy answers for me. Although I have never been a drinking or pill-popping woman, I have lately considered taking a shot of hard liquor and a couple of tranquilizers before trying to communicate with the 800 help- lines.

My call is always answered promptly and I am solemnly told that my call is important to them. The next available technician will be with me shortly, they say. I have sometimes sat for half an hour with a receiver glued to my newly forming cauliflower ear listening to repetitive, hysterical sounding sales pitches interspersed with maddeningly atonal, distorted canned music.

When the technician who is apparently just back from an extended trip, finally says he is ready to help me, and I have given him my name, address, telephone number, customer number and last four digits of my social security number, it turns out that I am talking to somebody in East Texas whereas I should be talking to somebody in West Texas and they will switch me over to them. This entails another long wait.

By the time the second technician answers I am in no mood for any advice beginning, "Look at your modem....."

"Listen," I interrupt him, "you are speaking to a ninety year old, non-technical lady who does not know a modem from a commode." (Actually I am exaggerating a little for dramatic effect I will not be ninety for another three months, but ninety sounds more impressive than a mere eighty nine.) "What I want is for you to send out somebody from your company to figure out what's wrong with my computer."

Although I hate to use this hard-boiled approach, I have found it effective a couple of times. I know it is not genteel; my mother would be horrified, and it embarrasses me that the technician is probably telling his cohorts, "You would not believe what some old biddy just said to me on the phone." But we do what we have to do.

The End of the World

I must tell you at the outset that I have always been an exceptionally fortunate person. This makes it difficult to account for what might seem to be the "Chicken Little" aspect of my nature. My family all think of me as a born worrier. I prefer to think of myself as a prudent old lady, a cautious investor, a concerned parent, a watchful grand-parent and great-grandparent (and soon-to-be great-great-grandparent), a loyal friend, and a conscientious dog-owner, not to mention a defensive driver, and a registered voter. In other words, I am someone who considers the what-ifs and maybes and probable pit-falls of life and tries to adjust matters accordingly.

Well, yes, I do have to keep a rein on my fertile, not to say febrile, imagination because given the opportunity I can conjure up some horrifying possibilities. However, for anyone who reads the paper or listens to news broadcasts, it is virtually impossible to avoid developing an unsettling, if not apocalyptic view, of our times. The realities often outstrip any horrors I might conjure up on my own.

Therefore, you can appreciate my consternation when I read not long ago that P.D. James, the eminent British mystery writer, stated her conviction that human beings will eventually go the way of the dodo. This is a possibility I had not yet considered.

Mind you, I pride myself on facing facts, scary though they may be. I have even made an effort to understand the concept of Singularity. Scientists tell us this is a condition in which technology will overtake and soon supersede human intelligence, thus making human beings obsolete. I checked out a massive tome from the library on the subject only to discover that I am already a victim of Singularity for which there is apparently no known cure. I have therefore resigned myself to being obsolete, which is not a good thing, but since it is a chronic condition, I have managed to accept it, just as I have learned to live with my trick knee.

However, it is one thing to become obsolete; becoming extinct is something else entirely!

P.D. James, who is in my own age group, is someone I greatly admire. From reading her brief autobiography a while back, I know she is a sensible, stalwart woman who has faced and overcome daunting problems in her personal life. She is a hugely successful author, a much-decorated and revered lady in Great Britain, and is seemingly as unlikely as Queen Elizabeth is to make sensational pronouncements or suffer an attack of the vapors. So when someone of her stature announces that human beings are on their way out altogether, it sounds pretty convincing.

So far as I know she did not give any specific date for when all of us might disappear.

This is a good thing. An open-ended prediction is surely preferable to the ones made by the elderly preacher who recently apologized for being wrong when he twice announced dates for the end of the world and neither one panned out. As he discovered to his regret, there is no sense in getting everybody riled up prematurely.

The nearest I have come to preparing for extinction is to have had my will up-dated recently. I might have worded things a bit differently had I known a mass human eradication was in the offing. Well, a person cannot anticipate every single detail.

I have not discussed any of this with my family because I am reluctant to upset them before I get all the facts lined up. I have noticed them studying me rather closely of late. I absolutely do not want to come across as a worry -wart or a crack-pot or some kind of control freak.

So I am turning my thoughts to happier things and planning what to plant in my garden. Spring is just around the corner----isn't it?

The Cure It Yourself Health Plan

When I was checking my ancient recipe file the other day, I ran across my mother's recipe for mustard plaster. It reminded me of the various home remedies often resorted to during my childhood. In those conservative, long-ago times, many families relied on a kind of cure-it-yourself health plan, with formal medical opinion asked for only when the sick or injured person's eyes began to glaze over.

Fortunately my mother was not that radical, but, on the other hand, neither did she hasten to call a doctor if one of us was ill or injured. After all, a three-dollar house call was a major expense, and she reasoned that most problems are not as bad as they might seem to be at first glance. Also, when confronted with any unfamiliar medical problem, mother had recourse to the nearest facility we had that was comparable to today's emergency room--- our next-door neighbors' house. An elderly German lady named Grandma Evis lived there with two adult daughters and her scholarly gentle-hearted son who was a hunchback.

Over the years of homesteading in a rugged and isolated area, while simultaneously managing to raise her six children to maturity, Grandma Evis had gradually earned great respect in the ranching community for her ability to not only diagnose ailments but to recommend effective home remedies to treat them. She had helped many to survive diseases ranging from influenza to tularemia, and had dealt with blood poisoning, gunshot wounds, bone fractures and snake-bite. After she retired to a comfortable home in Cheyenne, she became our family's health consultant and freely gave us the benefit of her hard-won knowledge. Ironically, the greatest regret of her life was that, although she had the ability to help so many others, she had been unable to effect a cure for her son's scoliosis, despite her years-long regimen of daily massage and stretching exercises to straighten his back.

One day when my brother suddenly broke out in an alarming display of itchy, puffy pink spots, he was hustled over to Grandma Evis who immediately explained that he was suffering from hives. She asked him if he had been eating anything different lately and he mentioned having had "quite a few apples." He had OD'd on the Jonathan apples mother kept stored in a bushel basket in our basement. Moderation in apple intake was advised and warm corn starch and baking soda baths were prescribed. The problem resolved within hours.

On another occasion my brother developed chilblains as a result of walking his paper route in sub-zero weather and then too quickly thawing out his numb feet by standing on the hot-air register in our dining room. Grandma Evis's miracle cure in this case was sliced raw onions liberally applied to the affected areas and held in place by his heavy socks. It is amazing how well this works and how long the essence of onion can linger in the atmosphere.

Under Grandma Evis's tutelage my mother became adept at making bread and milk poultices to draw out embedded splinters, flax seed poultices to promote healing of open sores, and mustard plasters to relieve the congestion of chest colds and pneumonia. She also learned to put drops of warmed mineral oil in my ears to alleviate the pain of my all too frequent earaches. (Once when the mineral oil treatment was insufficient, the family doctor was actually called. He had my mother hold an ether cone over my nose to anesthetize me while he lanced both of my ears.)

Our bathroom medicine cabinet also contained an array of standard medicines of the day which included aspirin tablets, mercurochrome, iodine, oil of cloves for toothaches, Epsom salts, castor oil, milk of magnesia, Mentholatum, Vicks Vaporub, Sloane's Liniment, Unguentine, for burns, and a tube of Ipana toothpaste to forestall the dreaded affliction referred to as "pink toothbrush." There were also rolls of gauze and rolls of adhesive tape (Bandaids had yet to be invented).

A small drawer held three hot water bottles and a supply of wool flannel cloths. If you have never had Vicks Vaporub dabbed around your nostrils and rubbed on your chest before a warmed piece of wool flannel was pinned to your pajama top and you were tucked into bed with a very hot water bottle at your feet, then I feel sorry for you. This, along with your mother's good night kiss, is one of the most comforting cold treatments known to human beings.

Stumbling Block

Periodicals devoted to the care, and general well-being of the geriatric population routinely remind us that falls are a foremost cause of permanent disability and death among the elderly. We are urged to check our homes for hazards underfoot and to make our lives safer by dispensing with throw rugs, by being aware of small objects left lying about that we might trip over, such as Fido's doggy chew-bone or even Fido himself. We are reminded to have adequate lighting if we need to get up in the night and to make certain we are oriented to our surroundings before trying to walk.

Whether we are indoors or outdoors, an assessment of our surroundings is essential before we make a move. Any tendency toward hasty or impromptu action should be nipped in the bud. The articles usually conclude by urging us to wear an alarm device at all times to summon help if we are perverse enough to have a fall anyway.

So, well, yes, I did have a fall. And no, I did not have an alarm device on me although I usually carry a cell phone when I am out in the yard. And yes, I did make an impulsive and somewhat tricky move. And no, I cannot blame anybody but myself for my injuries. (When you reach age ninety-one it doesn't behoove you to start pointing a finger at your guardian angel for each and every little lapse of attention. Angels get tired, too, you know.)

At four p.m. on the last Sunday in April I had just emptied a wastebasket in my trash bin and was returning up the front walkway to my house, when I noticed a plant in need of water. I grabbed a watering can, stepped up on a protruding rock in the wall surrounding the flower bed, lost my footing and fell backwards onto a broad concrete step.

It took about one second for me to realize I was in a serious predicament. I could not move without considerable pain and I was completely out of sight of any of my neighbors or any passersby on our quiet street. Although I am not a person who yells a lot, I still produced a few impressive bellows for help. When these did not have

135

any immediate result I decided to save my strength by shouting at intervals of every five minutes. An hour later, neighbors in two of the houses across the street heard me. After calling my son who called 911, they offered me all the comfort they could until help arrived and I was whisked off to the hospital for a three-week stay.

I had sustained a fractured left femur which was adroitly repaired by a young orthopedic surgeon who I am told bridged the break in my bone with a metal spike.

When I awoke after surgery, I found myself in bed, cozily nestled amongst pillows in a curtained, dimly lit space. I had no real idea where I was, but there was a glowing red button on my bed that said NURSE, so I pressed that. Two nurses popped up immediately.

"Pardon me," I said apologetically, "but I don't know exactly where I am. Is this by any chance Finland?"

I was calmly informed that no, I was not in Finland but in the transitional care unit of the Grass Valley hospital. I went back to sleep, but when the nurses looked in on me before going off duty the next morning, I remembered my goofy question and mentioned that I couldn't imagine why I'd asked something so silly. Both nurses smiled, and one of them reassured me that hallucinations are quite common among patients waking up after surgery.

Naturally I have mulled this matter over because I so like the world to make sense. I recalled that thirty years ago my husband and I took a trip to the Soviet Union. On our return journey we flew from Moscow to Helsinki, where we had a twenty-minute stopover before changing planes. I remember saying to my husband "Well, now I guess we can brag about visiting Finland. I wonder what it's really like"

My guess is that one of my remote and flickering brain cells was activated under anesthesia and what popped up was Finland. .My advice is to watch your step. One small miscalculation can send you some place you had no intention of going.

Are You Smiling?

In recent times, there has been a great deal of emphasis on the importance of nurturing a child's self-esteem. At first glance, this seems a direct contrast to the methods of child-rearing I recall from my formative years back in the 1920's and 1930's. My brother and I were sometimes reminded not to get "too uppity" or "too big for our britches," and were told on some occasions that "children should be seen and not heard." I do not remember that either one of us felt particularly damaged by these admonitions. (We noticed that almost everybody's parents seemed to say the same kind of things.) When we were spoken to in this way, we simply understood we had exceeded the bounds of acceptable behavior and that it would be advisable to "tone things down" as our father or mother suggested.

Furthermore it was ingrained in us that we were works in progress. Therefore we needed to pay attention because we had a lot to learn, and there was always plenty of room for improvement. We sometimes sighed under the weight of our parents' expectations and our teachers' demands for hard work and civil behavior. However, they were adults and we were children, and there was no blurring of our roles and no question at all about who was in charge.

As I think about this now, I realize my older brother and I, who were adopted children, were fortunate in our childhood. Ours was the kind of conservative small town upbringing that is now the stuff of Hallmark nostalgia. Life was far less complicated for us than it is for children today.

The pace was slower, the rules, even if not precisely defined, were still well understood and the boundaries agreed upon. For the most part, our growing up was allowed to be a gradual process.

Our play times were not organized or closely supervised, leaving us free to enjoy death-defying activities and hair-raising adventures as long as we didn't destroy property or maim each other, and providing that our mother knew our general whereabouts so that she could call us home to do our chores or run an errand to the corner grocery store.

We developed agility by climbing an old cottonwood tree to reach out for a rope that dangled six or eight feet above the ground. We then emulated Tarzan (I thought his full name was Tarzan of the Yapes) by swinging in a wide arc, hoping to make a lithe and graceful landing on the ground exactly the way Tarzan did it. We improved our balance by walking along high cement retaining walls with nothing to hang onto, and for a little extra excitement we skated on irregular downhill sidewalks wearing our clamp-on roller skates which loosened easily and caused some nasty falls. I had scabs on my knees all summer long.

Well, so times have changed, and it is easy for a very elderly person like me to exclaim, "Alas and alack! What is to become of the younger generation!" Everyday life now seems to me too constricted, too hurried, too complex, too impersonal, and, yes, too dangerous, to be a healthy environment for raising children.

When I see a knot of small children on the street corner waiting for the school bus, my first impulse is to pity them. These small commuters, burdened down by backpacks, appear equipped to enter a battle zone. They are regimented, poor things, and will never walk to school, kicking through fallen leaves or wading through snow drifts on the mile long trip the way I did.

Then I notice that as they await the bus, many of them are laughing and scuffling about as children have always done. And there are mothers or fathers sitting in cars, keeping an eye on the children, waiting to make certain their children are safely on the bus, before they go on to their daily routine.

Obviously far too many children are not cared for and guarded in this way, and even for those who are, childhood is not always the happy time it is touted to be. In fact, my experience has been that if you ask people if they would like to repeat their childhoods, they are apt to look thoughtful for a moment and then say, "Well, no, actually I wouldn't."

Growing up is very hard work. Helping a child grow into a compassionate and caring adult is a major achievement. Yes, let us foster self-esteem.

Counting by Tens

Ten years ago, when I turned eighty I wrote, with what I hoped was just the right note of nonchalance, that I was entering my eighth decade. Unfortunately I was wrong. I was then entering my ninth decade! This error was pointed out to me with the utmost kindness and tact by a careful reader who is also a perceptive editor. She explained that when one reaches age eighty, one has already lived eighty years or eight decades. Therefore, inevitably, the next step is into the ninth decade.

I accepted this incontrovertible logic with the rueful acknowledgment that once again my uncertain grasp of arithmetic had resulted in my reaching a false conclusion. I will admit that upping the decade count put a small dent in my bravado. For a while I seemed to see the words, "It is later than you think" written on the walls in my house. I went through a period when I obsessively practiced counting backwards from one hundred by threes in case I ever needed to be evaluated by a neurologist who I had been told sometimes used this as a quick test of mental competency.

Thank goodness my life gradually settled back into its usual channel and has flowed along since then without any particular turbulence if I discount annoying little memory lapses, a tendency to nod off while reading, diminished range of motion in practically all of my joints, and a total lack of enthusiasm for climbing hills or flights of stairs or anything else vertical. In my opinion there is nothing to be gained by making a statistical analysis of every little deviation from the norm. (In the first place who in the world gave some committee the right to set up norms for the rest of us to try to measure up to?)

Anyway, the other day when I was feeling particularly alert, organized and well-balanced, I made the mistake of deciding to look at next year's calendar in order to decide on exact dates for some of my projected activities. Alas, I was then brought face to face with my tenth decade! This milestone with a zero in it loomed large and cast a dark shadow.

Here I was, once again, confronted by the inexorable passing of time and I realized that I have far, far more time behind me than I have ahead of me. Not only that, but the slower I go, the faster time goes! I remember being taught something long ago about inverse relationships. I think I have just met up with one, and this is not a good thing.

When faced with unsettling and incontrovertible facts, I have found that it sometimes helps if one alters one's way of dealing with them.

What came to mind in this instance was how we played hide and go seek when I was a child. Whoever was "it" had to count to one hundred by ones to give everybody else enough time to find a hiding place. Counting by tens was strictly against the rules. As a way of stretching time, I have now decided to stop counting in decades and instead count in years.

The beauty of my scheme is that it allows me quite a bit of "wiggle" room. If I want to I can slow time even further by counting time in terms of months, weeks, days, hours, minutes or as a last resort, seconds.

I realize that at some point I will stop counting altogether, but I'm sure that will be all right. I surely will have fallen fast asleep because that's what I always do when I'm counting backwards by threes or counting sheep.

Birthdays
Accumulate,
The years accelerate,
Suddenly I find I'm doing
Ninety!

Curriculum Vitae

Lucille Lovestedt is a retired speech pathologist. During her tenure at Los Angeles County University of Southern California Medical Center, she was co-author of a professional paper and author of a workbook for aphasic patients, *Reclaiming Functional Communication,* Thomas Publishing Co.

Since her retirement to Grass Valley, California, she has been active in a writing group. Her short essays and articles have appeared in the *Grass Valley Union* newspaper, the *Sacramento Bee* and *Bark* magazine. One of her essays was selected for inclusion in the anthology *Open to All,* published by the Nevada County Library Association. She also won an honorable mention for a poem entered in one of the annual Writers Digest writing contests. She is also the author of an autobiographical novel, *Commission of Child and Animal Protection.*

20580642R00085

Made in the USA
Charleston, SC
18 July 2013